TEEN
SUICIDE

Other books in the At Issue series:

TEEN SUICIDE

John Woodward, *Book Editor*

Bruce Glassman, *Vice President*
Bonnie Szumski, *Publisher*
Helen Cothran, *Managing Editor*

GREENHAVEN PRESS
An imprint of Thomson Gale, a part of The Thomson Corporation

THOMSON
━━━━✦━━━━ ™
GALE

Detroit • New York • San Francisco • San Diego • New Haven, Conn.
Waterville, Maine • London • Munich

© 2005 Thomson Gale, a part of The Thomson Corporation.

Thomson and Star Logo are trademarks and Gale and Greenhaven Press are registered trademarks used herein under license.

For more information, contact
Greenhaven Press
27500 Drake Rd.
Farmington Hills, MI 48331-3535
Or you can visit our Internet site at http://www.gale.com

LIBRARY OF CONGRESS CATALOGING-IN-PUBLICATION DATA

Teen suicide / John Woodward, book editor.
     p. cm. — (At issue)
Includes bibliographical references and index.
ISBN 0-7377-2428-5 (lib. : alk. paper) — ISBN 0-7377-2429-3 (pbk. : alk. paper)
     1. Teenagers—Suicidal behavior—United States. 2. Teenagers—Mental health—United States. 3. Adolescent psychology—United States. 4. Suicide—United States—Prevention. I. Woodward, John, 1958– . II. At issue (San Diego, Calif.)
HV6546.T414 2005
362.28'0835'0973—dc22   2004042427

Printed in the United States of America

Contents

Introduction

On January 6, 2002, fifteen-year-old Charles Bishop intentionally flew a Cessna 172-R into the twenty-eighth floor of the Bank of America building in Tampa, Florida, killing himself. Covered by newspapers and television around the world, it was a highly dramatic symbol of a surprisingly common act—teen suicide. Even when a teen suicide is less public, however, it still has profound effects on parents, siblings, friends, teachers, and the broader community. According to social worker Jon Connelly, "The death of a loved one hurts. The death of a child hurts even more. The death of a child by suicide causes horrible and lasting pain affecting parents, siblings, grandparents, friends, teachers, and others."

There are many adult suicides each year, some of which may be prompted by mental illness, divorce, financial difficulties, terminal illness, or criminal behavior. But it is not a leading cause of adult deaths. Suicide is, however, a leading cause of death among teenagers. After unintentional injury and homicide, suicide is the leading cause of death for Americans between the ages of fifteen and twenty-four. Female teens are more likely to attempt suicide, but teen males are four times more likely to actually complete the act.

In addition, the teen suicide rate has been on the rise for decades. From 1952 to 1995, the incidence of suicide among adolescents and young adults nearly tripled. From 1980 to 1997, the rate of suicide among persons aged fifteen to nineteen years increased by 11% and among persons aged ten to fourteen years by 109 percent. In 1998 more teenagers and young adults died from suicide than from cancer, heart disease, AIDS, birth defects, stroke, pneumonia and influenza, and chronic lung disease combined. Each year, more than five thousand young people between the ages of fifteen to twenty-four commit suicide. An additional 1.2 million young people attempt suicide each year. But even these alarming statistics fail to tell the whole story of the impact of teen suicide—particularly the impact on the survivors. Writer Carol J. Van Dongen states, "Survivors of suicide, that is, the relatives and friends of the person who commits suicide, are generally viewed as a vulnerable population at high risk for suffering disturbances in physical and psychological functioning. . . . Most survivors of suicide are left with an emotional burden and unfinished business related to the death, plus uncertainty regarding how the suicide could continue to affect their lives."

It has often been said that the greatest loss parents can suffer is the death of one of their children. When the death of a child is by suicide, the parents' shock and surprise can be overwhelming. It is a loss of such magnitude that the parents of suicide victims often entertain suicidal thoughts themselves. They also suffer from more than grief over their loss. Invariably, the parents feel guilt for not having seen the warning signs of suicide that would have allowed them to prevent it. According to author Antoinette Bosco, "Among the questions that always come up to haunt us, [those] who have lost a loved one to suicide, is: Couldn't you see the signs or clues that indicated their desperation? That question is a cruel one for the survivors who must now live with the tragedy of suicide for the rest of their lives."

Compounding their pain, the parents of teen suicide victims may even feel shame due to the societal stigma attached to suicide. According to researcher Julie Cerel, "For survivors of suicide, social support may be reduced because of the stigma associated with suicide. In many religious traditions, suicide has been stigmatized, and the death is treated differently by the community." There are many instances in which the parents of a child suicide victim become isolated and ostracized. In one case, after a sixteen-year-old boy took his own life, his grieving single mother noticed that people in town treated her differently. In an attempt to keep his memory alive, she tried to remain connected to others in her son's life. However, when she attended some graduation parties for her son's friends, she noticed that people stiffened when they saw her. Nobody knew what to say to her. As a result, she stopped going to the parties and began to spend most of her time alone. She believed her life had been ruined and began to suffer from clinical depression. Eventually, however, like many other parents of suicide victims, she was able to redirect her grief into a positive force by volunteering with organizations dedicated to the prevention of teen suicide.

The brothers and sisters of teen suicide victims also suffer. Author Michelle Linn-Gust, who wrote the suicide sibling survivor guide, *Do They Have Bad Days in Heaven?* in response to her own sister's suicide, explains, "Sibling survivors are often called the forgotten mourners. . . . Because of the suicide, the surviving siblings' roles in the family are altered. They might feel the need to parent their parents or protect them from anything else bad happening. The opposite could also happen where the parents try to shield the living children, afraid of losing them, too." Sibling survivors can become confused and gravely depressed themselves. They may struggle to gain a mature understanding of death. They may retreat into their own sadness, fear, and anxiety, and when their parents inevitably become overprotective to prevent another suicide, they may rebel. The sense of safety and routine that children depend on in the family's daily life is shattered; hope for the future is replaced by gloom and foreboding. Tragically, they may even be tempted to follow in the victim's footsteps. Suicide researchers have found greater rates of suicidal behavior in the relatives of suicides.

The impact of a teen suicide extends beyond the victim's family. The victim's friends suffer from grief and frequently also from guilt due to their failure to tell an adult of their knowledge of the victim's anguish in the days leading up to the act. Suicide researchers David Brent and Rebecca Conobbio conducted a study on the impact of teen suicide on surviving friends and found that "29% of the friends of suicide victims had a . . . major depressive episode within six months of the death of their friend." Of special concern is that one teen suicide can result in others.

Teen suicide victims are often memorialized by schools and communities in an attempt to bring closure to schoolmates and friends. Such memorials, however, as well as excessive media coverage, can inspire copycats who yearn for the sympathy and attention lavished on the victim, and this can lead to suicide clusters. Teenagers have long been attracted to the romanticization of suicide in literature and films, from *Romeo and Juliet* to *Ordinary People*. After a teen suicide, the local teen suicide rate tends to increase in proportion to the volume and frequency of the coverage of the event by television and newspapers. According to Ellen McGinnis-Smith, Des Moines schools' deputy director of student and family services, "After a suicide you have to watch very carefully that you do not have more. It is of concern that there could be copycat suicides. If kids get an idea it's glorified, they can be impulsive. We need to be very careful."

The teachers of a teen suicide victim are also impacted. The school environment becomes dark; students can become morbidly fascinated with the victim and the method of suicide. Teachers are forced to become more vigilant in an effort to ward off additional deaths; students may find this increased scrutiny invasive. Teachers must also help students cope with the tragedy, something their training has not necessarily equipped them to do. Author Elizabeth Gleick describes the impact on teachers and students of the suicide of a teenaged girl named Alicia:

> Denise Marovich-Sampson, an English teacher who coordi-nates the impact counseling program, which consists mostly of voluntary discussion groups, says Alicia was re-ferred to her, but refused to attend impact sessions. "I have this guilt thing, thinking, did I do enough? But yeah, I did," says Marovich-Sampson. "If a child is not willing to get help, I can't drag her out of class kicking and screaming."

The impact on the school was greatest in the first day after the tragedy. "Students clustered in hallways weeping; classes sat numb and silent; teachers broke down at an after-school meeting. Says [a] math teacher: 'It was the roughest teaching day I've ever had.'"

Teen suicide affects more than just the victims—its impact ripples outward from a single home to the entire community. As a result, the re-cent increase in the number of teen suicides has led society to struggle to understand the root causes of teen suicide and to work diligently to de-velop approaches to prevent it. In recent years, the federal government has become involved. U.S. surgeon general David Satcher called for a na-tional strategy to prevent suicide, including teen suicide. Senator Christo-pher Dodd made the prevention of teen and young adult suicide his first priority as chairman of the Senate Subcommittee on Children and Fami-lies. In addition, the number of hotlines and Web sites related to teen sui-cide is large and increasing. These and other developments reflect grow-ing national recognition of the seriousness of the problem.

Scientists and social critics have looked at a variety of contributing factors to the rise of teen suicide. They may strongly disagree with one an-other as they argue for or against a particular cause or solution, but they all agree on one thing: Teen suicide is a tragic waste that negatively af-fects everyone touched by it. The following viewpoints in *At Issue: Teen Suicide* represent some of the current thinking about what parents, friends, teachers, and society can do to prevent teen suicide.

1

Teen Suicide Is a Serious Problem

David Satcher

David Satcher was surgeon general of the United States from 1998 to 2002.

Between 1952 and 1994, teen suicide in the United States tripled, and in 2001 suicide was the third leading cause of death of young Americans. Minorities are increasingly victims of suicide. Between 1980 and 1994, suicide among young black males doubled, and American Indians/Alaska Natives commit suicide at a higher rate than any other group in the country. The U.S. Centers for Disease Control is now proactive in attempting to prevent teen and young adult suicide through promoting awareness, surveillance, research, and the implementation and evaluation of suicide screening and prevention programs.

Editor's Note: The following viewpoint was originally given as testimony before the Senate Health, Education, Labor, and Pensions Subcommittee on Children and Families.

As you know, suicide is a major problem in this country. Approximately 31,000 Americans kill themselves each year and hundreds of thousands more who have attempted suicide fill our emergency rooms each day. In 1998, it was the 8th leading cause of death in this country and the third leading cause of death for adolescents and young adults. While suicide rates have been declining modestly since the mid 1990's, preliminary 1999 statistics indicate that about the same number of teenagers and young adults die from suicide as from the next 7 leading causes of death, which include cancer, heart disease, AIDS, birth defects, stroke, pneumonia and influenza, and chronic lung disease, combined.

The scars from suicide run deep and wide. Family members, classmates, friends, and entire communities feel the devastating impact of a life taken by suicide. While every suicide is tragic, the news of a young person, whose life has hardly begun, dying by suicide, is especially heart-felt.

The overriding tragedy in all of this is that so many suicides are pre-

David Satcher, testimony before the Subcommittee on Children and Families, Senate Committee on Health, Education, Labor, and Pensions, Washington, DC, September 7, 2001.

ventable. But the myths and misconceptions surrounding suicide have led people to believe that suicide is an inexplicable act. It is estimated that 90 to 95 percent of suicides are associated with a history of mental illness, usually depression—a treatable disease. Of greater concern is the fact that many health professionals do not recognize suicide as a preventable cause of death.

The public health approach to youth suicidal behavior prevention

In public health, we approach the problem of youth suicidal behavior by asking four questions:
1. *What is the problem? (Surveillance).* We collect data on the problem that we can use to better understand the problem and to do something about it. We ask "where, when, and why did it happen, and to whom?"
2. *What are the causes? (Risk or Protective Factor Research).* We seek to discover what puts people at risk or protects them.
3. *What works to help prevent the problem? (Intervention Evaluation).* We use the knowledge we have of the pattern of the problem to develop and test interventions that might work to prevent it.
4. *How do you do it? (Program Implementation).* We look at how we can accelerate the dissemination of research findings more quickly and effectively. We also explore how we apply the proven interventions broadly in the community in safe and effective ways.

The continued prominence of suicide and attempted suicide among our youth as a leading cause of death and injury is an urgent problem. It is more important than ever that we apply our resources in the most efficient manner possible. Emphasis by the Office of the Surgeon General during my tenure, as well as by others, on a public health approach has allowed many more partners from the public and private sectors, representing states, communities, schools, grassroots organizations, parents, researchers, clinicians, and more to contribute to the solution to this pressing problem. The public health efforts focus on prevention, are science-based, and integrate the approaches and findings of many different fields and disciplines. We have learned a number of things in public health that can help.

What we know about the problem of youth suicidal behavior

Assessing the Problem

It is important for us to begin by taking a closer look at this problem based on what we have learned from surveillance and research. Suicide remains the third leading cause of death for young people in the U.S., between the ages of 10 and 24 years. Males under the age of 25 are much more likely to die by suicide than their female counterparts. The 1998 sex ratio for people aged 15–19 was 5:1 (males to females), while among those aged 20–24 it was 6:1. Firearms (60%) and hanging (26%) were the two most common methods of suicide used by persons aged 10–24 years. From 1952–1994, the incidence of suicide among adolescents and young adults nearly tripled. Although there has been a slight decline in youth suicides since 1994, the number of young people who die by suicide, particularly by firearms, remains unacceptably high—indeed, any single suicide is unacceptable. An international comparison of suicide among adolescents and young adults aged 15–24 years in 34 of the wealthiest nations showed that the United States had the second highest rate of firearm-related suicide and had the 12th highest rate overall. Any consideration of suicide must also include the emotional, psychological, and economic impact of any suicide on families, friends, and communities.

Not unlike many of the other public health problems confronting the country today, significant disparities exist in the area of suicide. From 1980 to 1994, suicide doubled in young black males 15–19 years old. Dr. Alvin Poussaint, in his recent book, *Lay My Burden Down: Unraveling Suicide and the Mental Health Crisis Among African-Americans*, includes in his definition of "suicide," such fatal self-destructive behaviors as alcohol and drug abuse, victim-perpetrated homicide, and "suicide by cop," e.g., assaulting or provoking police officers in a way that serves to lead the officer to use deadly force. His perspective highlights the additional morbidity and mortality suffered by many of the Nation's minority youth.

It is estimated that 90 to 95 percent of suicides are associated with a history of mental illness, usually depression—a treatable disease.

American Indians/Alaska Natives 15–24 years of age die by suicide at a higher rate than the rest of the population. We need increased surveillance in this area. Some studies show suicide rates in some Native communities more than three times the national rate. While we know that alcoholism and drug dependency are major problems in some of these communities at risk, and that they are also major risk factors for suicide, we need to understand why other Native communities seem protected against these problems. As we recently highlighted in the Culture, Race and Ethnicity supplement to the Mental Health Report, suicide rates vary widely among ethnic minority groups in the United States, and it is incumbent upon us to learn more about what protects against suicide for some groups and what increases risk for others.

The Centers for Disease Control and Prevention (CDC), the U.S. Department of Education, Department of Justice, and the National School Safety Center have examined homicides and suicides associated with schools and identified common features of school-related violent deaths. The study examined events on both public and private school property which occurred as a person was going to and from school, or while someone was on the way or going to an official school-sponsored event. Over nearly a decade, the data show that 15 percent of school-associated deaths are suicides. The study also found that, in some cases, youth who are assaultive at school are also suicidal.

The magnitude of the burden of suicidal behavior cannot be appreciated by only examining the deaths. The number of completed suicides reflects only a small portion of the impact of suicidal behavior. It is estimated that more people are hospitalized due to suicide attempts than are fatally injured, and an even greater number of people attempt suicide and are treated in ambulatory settings or are not treated at all. In 1987, the state legislature in Oregon mandated that hospitals treating a child aged less than 18 years for injuries resulting from a suicide attempt report the attempt to the State Health Division. Using information from that system, it was estimated that for the years 1997–1999 for every one suicide among that age group there are approximately 45 suicide attempts.

The continued prominence of suicide and attempted suicide among our youth as a leading cause of death and injury is an urgent problem.

CDC continually monitors behaviors among youth that have an impact on their health through a surveillance system, the Youth Risk Behavior Survey (YRBS), conducted in collaboration with the States. This survey is administered to high school students in grades 9–12. Part of this survey covers risk behaviors for suicidal-related injuries and deaths. In 1999 (the latest year for which these data are available), the YRBS showed that during the 12 months preceding the survey: 19.3 percent of students (about one out of every five) in grades 9–12 had seriously considered suicide; 14.5 percent of students had made a specific plan to attempt suicide; 8.3 percent (about one out of every 13 students or 1.3 million) had made an attempt one or more times; and 2.6 percent sustained injuries during a suicide attempt that required medical treatment. In contrast to suicides, where males have the highest rates, studies of suicidal thoughts and suicide attempts routinely show females with higher rates. A recent trend analysis of the data on suicidal ideation and behavior during the years 1991–1997 showed that while the percentage of students seriously considering suicide and those who made a suicide plan was decreasing, the number of injurious attempt had increased. This may indicate that students who attempt are less likely to die but more likely to suffer serious injury. A 1995, national survey of college students, the National College Health Risk Behavior Survey, found that in the 12 months preceding the survey, one in ten had seriously considered suicide and approximately one in every sixty-seven had attempted suicide.

Risk and Protective Factors Research Findings

People have a great many misconceptions about suicide. One of the most impeding misconceptions is that suicide is an inexplicable act; in reality, many known risk factors exist.

From analysis of data on youth suicidal behavior, we know that:

- Attempted suicide among adolescents is a disturbingly frequent event. Adolescents and young adults report attempting suicide at much higher percentages than middle aged or elderly adults. Survivors of suicide attempts are at higher risk of subsequently completing suicide.
- Impulsivity is often associated with adolescent suicide attempts.
- Relatively few studies have examined protective factors among youth for suicidal behavior. Both parent-family connectedness and

perceived school connectedness have been shown to be protective against suicidal behavior.

In reviewing research on youth suicidal behavior, we have identified the following risk factors:

- Biopsychosocial Risk Factors
  - Mental disorders, particularly mood disorders, schizophrenia, anxiety disorders and certain personality disorders
  - Alcohol and other substance use disorders
  - Hopelessness
  - Impulsive and/or aggressive tendencies
  - History of trauma or abuse
  - Some major physical illnesses
  - Family history of suicide
- Environmental Risk Factors
  - Job or financial loss
  - Relational or social loss
  - Easy access to lethal means
  - Exposure to others who have died by suicide
- Sociocultural Risk Factors
  - Lack of social support and a sense of isolation
  - Stigma associated with help-seeking behavior
  - Barriers to accessing health care, especially mental health and substance abuse treatment
  - Certain cultural and religious beliefs (for instance, the belief that suicide is a noble resolution of a personal dilemma)
  - Exposure to, including through the media, and influence of others who have died by suicide

There are also important effective protective factors:

- Effective clinical care for mental, physical, and substance use disorders
- Easy access to a variety of clinical interventions and support for help-seeking
- Restricted access to highly lethal means of suicide
- Strong connections to family and community support
- Support through ongoing medical and mental health care relationships
- Skills in problem solving, conflict resolution, and nonviolent handling of disputes
- Cultural and religious beliefs that discourage suicide and support self-preservation

Successful strategies and programs

Intervention Evaluation

A 1999 report from the Institute of Medicine, entitled Reducing the Burden of Injury 1999: Advancing Prevention and Treatment, pointed to the need for evaluating programs: "The major challenge for research is the development and testing of new interventions to prevent suicide. Research on the prevention of suicide clearly warrants higher priority from the Department of Health and Human Services. . . ."

In fiscal year 1998, Congress provided funds to CDC for research to determine what interventions work to prevent suicidal behavior. One of these projects was focused on adolescents. Below is a brief summary:

- Research Foundation for Mental Hygiene connected to Columbia University is evaluating a program among high school students. The program is designed to enhance awareness, utilization, and efficacy of telephone crisis intervention services for teenagers. Students will be assessed on their use and perceptions of various kinds of treatment services and help-seeking behavior. The intervention augments an existing health curriculum and introduces a crisis line phone number. Students' calls to the line will be tracked. Initial findings show that high school students are willing to seek health-related assistance from a number of sources with questionable ability to provide the help they need.

- A new initiative to be awarded in FY [fiscal year] 2001, "Cooperative Agreements to Improve and Evaluate Crisis Hotlines," calls for certification of 200–300 crisis programs in the management of callers expressing suicidal thoughts or behaviors. These certified programs are to be networked through telephone technology that will permit national access to crisis center/hotline services through a single toll-free number. This three-year, $9 million initiative also seeks to evaluate the effectiveness of crisis centers and hotlines in reducing suicide risk. This is an area of study where extant research is equivocal in its findings.

Program Implementation

Two years ago, we released the Surgeon General's Call to Action to Prevent Suicide. In it, we laid out a three-pronged approach to preventing suicide using the acronym AIM—A for Awareness, which is aimed at increasing public awareness of suicide and its risk factors. I for Intervention, which called for enhancing the services and programs to prevent suicide. And M for Methodology, which spelled out the need for more research to understand the risk and protective factors of suicide.

Males under the age of 25 are much more likely to die by suicide than their female counterparts.

We pointed out that suicide prevention is everybody's business. We called for broad-based involvement from educators, health care professionals, the criminal justice system, substance abuse and treatment providers, churches and other faith-based organizations, community organizations, and the media. Since then, people in communities all across the country started getting busy and developing their own action agendas to address this problem. Needless to say, I have been pleased with the way the American people have responded.

Three months ago, we issued the National Strategy to Prevent Suicide to bring about social change needed to prevent suicide and reduce suicidal behaviors. It is the result of extensive collaboration with partners in the public and private sectors, culminating with four public hearings to listen to those most affected by suicide. The strategy is not a federal plan—it is a national plan designed to further the dialogue and action that has already begun in communities across the country and to serve as a springboard for changing attitudes, policies, and services.

Successful implementation of the National Strategy's 11 goals will aid in achieving the suicide prevention objectives outlined in Healthy People 2010, the nation's public health agenda.

- Promote awareness that suicide is a public health problem that is preventable.
- Develop broad-based support for suicide prevention.
- Develop and implement strategies to reduce the stigma associated with being a consumer of mental health, substance abuse, and suicide prevention services.
- Development and implement community-based suicide prevention programs.
- Promote efforts to reduce access to lethal means and methods of self-harm.
- Implement training for recognition of at-risk behavior and delivery of effective treatment.
- Develop and promote effective clinical and professional practices and substance abuse services.
- Increase access to and community linkages with mental health and substance abuse services.
- Improve reporting and portrayals of suicidal behavior, mental illness, and substance abuse in the entertainment and news media.
- Promote and support research on suicide and suicide prevention.
- Improve and expand surveillance systems.

The strategy recognizes the value and synergy of a community-based or population based approach, such as that used by the Air Force for the past five years. This approach seeks to enhance protective factors through mentoring programs and life skills enrichment. In conjunction, interventions are specifically targeted to those identified as being at risk, e.g., ensuring access to effective mental health treatment. The ultimate goal is a society where protective factors are more prevalent and risk factors less prevalent, so fewer people come to the point where they must be rescued from the brink of despair.

In collaboration with NIH [National Institutes of Health] and CDC, the Center for Mental Health Services has developed a comprehensive suicide prevention website containing a wealth of information. This resource is rich with information and can be found at www.mentalhealth.org/suicideprevention.

Future directions for moving forward together

We believe that the public health approach can help focus investments in preventing suicidal behavior if programs are founded on good evidence.

Throughout my testimony, I have used the public health framework to address the problem of adolescent and young adult suicide. I would like to return to this framework to set out some future directions that we can take together to address this problem.

Awareness
- In order to mobilize social and political will, it is necessary for the public to understand that many suicides are preventable—that in-

dividuals who want to take their own lives can be helped. The situation is not hopeless. Both federal agencies, such as the National Institutes of Health (NIH) and the Substance Abuse and Mental Health Services Agency (SAMHSA), and private organizations have developed educational efforts to explain the role of mental illness and substance abuse in suicide risk. However, the recent tragic event in Seattle, where commuters were encouraging a young woman to jump to her death, clearly highlights the need for a more informed public. We envision a day when people are as aware of the signs of suicide risk and steps to prevention as they are aware of CPR [Cardiopulmonary Resuscitation].

Surveillance

- *The National Violent Death Reporting System.* NVDRS is a state-based system for providing detailed information about violent deaths, including suicide, such as when they happen, where they happen, and how they happen. This information can be used to design and evaluate prevention strategies throughout the United States. Current systems for collecting information about suicide and other violent deaths do not include the circumstances around the death, or pertinent details about the means used.

Implementation and Evaluation

- *State and local suicide prevention.* About half of our state governments are involved in suicide prevention at some level. Because suicide prevention requires a multi-pronged approach, the common challenge is to coordinate across multiple arms of government, such as education, mental health, public health, and justice. Federal support for such coordination through technical assistance and funding would give states important help in providing suicide prevention leadership and programs to their communities.

- *Evaluation of youth suicide prevention programs.* While NIH and the CDC have supported research evaluating several approaches to reducing suicidal behavior among youth seen in emergency rooms or mental health clinics, there remains a need for evaluation of broader programs. Currently, many schools either have programs that are not based on the best scientific knowledge, or are implementing proven programs in ways other than as designed. We need to provide more support to communities in identifying and implementing best practice interventions. Typically, these are school-based and, in ideal circumstances, integrate other community resources such as the health care, faith-based organizations, and juvenile justice system. Evaluation research on these community-based programs is one of our most pressing needs.

- *Technical Resource Center.* An objective in the National Strategy calls for a Technical Resource Center consisting of several components, including a toll free information and referral service, an Internet website, a communication plan for informing various audiences about the Center, and technical assistance. The toll free information and referral service will provide a single point of access to Federal information about suicide and suicidal behavior. In addition, the information line will work toward raising awareness of suicide prevention while providing target audiences with materials to aid them in their work at the local, state, and national levels. The website will serve as a portal to existing federal agencies websites and link directly to Federal Reports, brochures and resources, and other links with suicide information. The Internet site will have high quality, interactive information such as news, funding opportunities in the Federal government, references, publications, calendar of events, and so on. The communication plan will develop strategies for marketing and promoting the toll free information line and website, and promoting distribution of suicide prevention materials developed by all Federal Agencies such as the National Strategy for Suicide Prevention. Additionally, technical assistance will be provided to key constituencies in the development of intervention and prevention programs.

Research

- Although our knowledge base has grown significantly over the past decade, some areas urgently need more study. For instance, we need to evaluate programs for their influence on suicidal behaviors that have already been proven effective in preventing violence and substance abuse. We also need to examine the benefits of interventions for depression and other mental disorders among young people. We need more community-based research to better understand the community factors that protect against or increase risk factors for suicide and learn how to change those factors toward protection. Still, a growing science base now allows us to move forward judiciously to implement these community-based suicide prevention initiatives, evaluating our efforts every step of the way, and seizing every opportunity to make programs more effective. . . .

I am honored to have this opportunity to bring you the public health perspective on addressing the problem of suicidal behavior among our youth and to share with you some of the things we have learned. We can be encouraged by modest declines in youth suicide rates between 1994 and 1998; but we cannot afford to be complacent. We have no reason to believe youth suicide will go away without a prolonged prevention campaign. We must fundamentally change the way our society approaches building resiliency and community connectedness in our young people, as well as how we respond to suicidal thoughts and suicidal acts. Suicide is among our most complex and persistent public health problems, not unlike tobacco use, teen pregnancy, and drug and alcohol abuse. There is no simple solution. If we are serious about addressing this issue, we must significantly step up our level of activity in suicide prevention.

2

Gay Teens Are at Greater Risk of Suicide

Gary Remafedi

Gary Remafedi is on the faculty of the University of Minnesota Medical School in Minneapolis.

A controversial 1989 report concluded that gay youths were two to three times more likely to attempt suicide than other young people. However, some researchers claimed that there was no population-based evidence linking sexual orientation and suicide. To date, several peer-reviewed studies have indeed found high rates of suicide attempts among young bisexual and homosexual research volunteers. Other studies have found a strong connection between suicide attempts and substance abuse and mental health symptoms in gay, lesbian, and bisexual youths. Mental health experts should now recognize that there is an increased risk of suicide among gay youths and work to save their lives.

O ver the past 25 years, researchers have reported consistently high rates of suicidality among homosexual persons, particularly among adolescents and young adults. Based on the data available at the time, the 1989 Report of the Secretary's Task Force on Youth Suicide concluded that "gay youth are 2 to 3 times more likely to attempt suicide than other young people. They may comprise up to 30% of completed youth suicides annually."

The report ignited a controversy that has persisted to the present day. In response to public and congressional inquiries, the American Association of Suicidology, Washington, DC, the Centers for Disease Control and Prevention, Atlanta, GA, and the National Institute of Mental Health, Rockville, MD, convened a workshop in 1994 regarding rates of suicide among gay men and lesbians. Some of the meeting attendees concluded that "there is no population-based evidence that sexual orientation and suicidality are linked in some direct or indirect manner." However, in light of the research published soon thereafter, that judgment might have been premature and overstated.

To date, at least 10 peer-reviewed studies have found unusually high

Gary Remafedi, "Suicide and Sexual Orientation: Nearing the End of Controversy?" *Archives of General Psychiatry*, vol. 56, October 1999, p. 885. Copyright © 1999 by the American Medical Association. Reproduced by permission.

rates of attempted suicide, in the range of 20% to 42%, among young bi-sexual and homosexual research volunteers. Additionally, 6 other population-based and controlled studies published since 1997 have cor-roborated the findings from volunteers. All have found a clinically and statistically significant association between suicide attempts and homo-sexuality, strongest among males.

The 2 new articles in this issue of the ARCHIVES by Fergusson et al and Herrell et al are the latest additions to the mounting evidence of a strong link between homosexuality and suicide. Herrell and coauthors analyzed data on suicidality and same-sex sexual behavior from a unique database of male, military veteran twin pairs. . . .

The investigators found that men with same-gender sexual partners were 6.5 times as likely as their co-twins to have attempted suicide, and the relatively high risk was not explained by mental health or substance abuse disorders.

At least 3 previous studies have found a significant association be-tween reported suicide attempts and substance abuse or mental health symptoms in gay, lesbian, and bisexual (GLB) youth, and several others have noted that GLB youth were more likely than heterosexual youth to abuse substances or to suffer from mental health symptoms. However, the veteran's database study is 1 of only 2 studies to have shown that the association between suicidality and same-gender sexual orientation in men is independent of the confounding effects of substance abuse and mental health diagnoses.

To date, at least 10 peer-reviewed studies have found unusually high rates of attempted suicide, in the range of 20% to 42%, among young bisexual and homosexual research volunteers.

The other study, by Fergusson et al, examined the extent to which 28 GLB youth in a New Zealand birth cohort were at risk of suicidal behav-iors and psychiatric disorders . . . The GLB youths were found to be at in-creased risk of a variety of psychiatric disorders, nicotine dependence, and suicidal ideation and attempts. The odds of a suicide attempt among homosexual persons from the 2 studies in this issue were quite similar and closely resemble figures from a population-based study of Minnesota students.

The current articles have similar strengths pertaining to the unique samples and systematic assessment of psychiatric symptoms. The co-twins in the veteran database study serve as exceptionally well-matched controls for many of the hereditary and environmental factors that can influence suicidality. The Christchurch Health and Development Study is a 21-year longitudinal study of 1265 children born in Christchurch, New Zealand. The use of these rare databases averted some of the potential biases asso-ciated with prior convenience samples. Both of the current studies gath-ered data through face-to-face or telephone interviews, a methodological departure from, and possible improvement on, the more commonly used written surveys.

If not for mental health problems, what can explain the high prevalence of suicide attempts among young homosexual persons? The veteran database study could not directly compare the odds of suicidality among monozygotic and dizygotic twins because of insufficient numbers of sexually discordant pairs. However, there was no association between suicidality and zygosity in the regression analyses, as might be expected if heritable mental illness or other biological conditions were at play.

At least 3 previous studies have found a significant association between reported suicide attempts and substance abuse or mental health symptoms in gay, lesbian, and bisexual (GLB) youth.

Although the current studies were not specifically designed to identify comorbities, 6 prior studies comparing homosexually oriented suicide attemptors with nonattemptors highlighted social risk factors such as gender nonconformity, early awareness of homosexuality, gay-related stress, victimization by violence, lack of social support, school dropout, family problems, suicide attempts by friends or relatives, and homelessness. Based on the results of the current studies, there appears to have been no decline in the risk of suicide for GLB individuals born from 1949 (the mean birth year of the veteran database sample) to 1977 (the birth year of the Christchurch Health and Development Study sample). As the authors of the twin study allude, whatever societal progress has been made in the interim might not have benefited adolescents struggling with the issue of sexual orientation.

In addition to their strengths, the current studies also share some common limitations. Like many prior studies, these studies could not examine sex differences. Women were not represented in the veteran database, and there were too few GLB subjects in the Christchurch Health and Development Study for statistical analysis of sex differences. Although adolescent women in the general population attempt suicide more often than adolescent men, young lesbian women and homosexual men have been found to have similarly high rates of attempted suicide. Two recently published studies of large, representative student populations in Minnesota and Massachusetts found suicide attempts to be associated with homosexuality in boys but not girls. Apparently, a homosexual orientation does not compound the already greater risk of suicide attempts for women compared with men.

Another prominent gap in all of the existing research is an examination of ethnic and racial differences. As illustrated by the current studies, the percentage of self-identifying homosexual persons in the general population is so small that relatively huge samples are needed for meaningful subpopulation analyses. It is imperative that future large-scale population surveys include questions about sexual orientation and oversample minority groups to represent them appropriately.

Both of the current studies focus on special populations defined by military service or birth in Christchurch, limiting the generalizability of the findings to other places and types of persons. However, taken together with earlier studies, there can be little doubt about the conclusion that homosexual orientation is associated with suicidality, at least among young men. Whether the risk of suicide peaks during adolescence, as expected, or remains constant throughout the life cycle is still unknown. Moreover, the extent to which suicide attempts in homosexual persons result in actual deaths remains to be determined. Although 2 psychological autopsy studies have investigated the sexuality of suicide victims, sexual orientation is difficult to determine posthumously, and the prior studies' findings have been hard to interpret.

It is time to put the controversy aside and be about the business of saving lives.

Certainly, there is much more to be learned about the circumstances and causes of attempted and completed suicide among homosexual people. Understanding the link between suicide and sexual orientation may provide important new clues to the general problem of youth suicide. As we continue to gather new information from studies such as the two in this issue, suicidologists and psychiatrists should recognize the serious risk of suicide facing some GLB people. The evidence is sufficiently compelling to warrant the education of mental health professionals as well as the development of preventive interventions for GLB youths. It is time to put the controversy aside and be about the business of saving lives.

3

The Gay Teen Suicide Epidemic Is a Myth

Traditional Values Coalition

Traditional Values Coalition is an interdenominational public policy organization comprising over forty-three thousand member churches.

For years, homosexual activists have claimed that 30 percent of all teen suicide victims are gay. This claim is based on a faulty research report published by Paul Gibson in 1989. In fact, gay teens are no more likely to commit suicide than nongay teens. Despite the fact that more recent studies have demonstrated the flaws in Gibson's study, homosexual activists continue to use the 30 percent myth to convince public school officials to establish prohomosexual counseling programs, gay clubs, and antihomophobia training sessions to convince straight students to accept homosexuality.

For more than a decade, Traditional Values Coalition has been repeatedly exposing the myth of an "epidemic" of "homosexual" teen suicides.

Now, a psychologist has published the results of two studies that—once again—expose the Homosexual Urban Legend that teens who have homosexual feelings are committing suicides in record numbers.

The 30% myth

Homosexual activists have repeatedly claimed for more than ten years that 30% of all teens who have attempted suicide are homosexuals. The mythological 30% figure was concocted by a homosexual social worker named Paul Gibson who wrote "Gay Male and Lesbian Youth Suicide," published in 1989. It has been thoroughly debunked, but homosexuals continue to use the figure because it supports their political and social agenda.

This 30% myth has been used over and over again to convince public school officials to establish pro-homosexual counseling programs, special clubs for homosexuals run by Gay, Lesbian, and Straight Education Network (GLSEN) teenagers, and sensitivity/anti-homophobia training sessions to convince straight students that homosexual behavior is normal.

The latest studies that expose the 30% urban legend appear in the December, 2001 issue of *Journal of Consulting and Clinical Psychology*. The author of these studies is Cornell University psychologist Ritch Savin-Williams.

Savin-Williams says previous homosexual teen suicide studies were flawed and exaggerated because they were drawn from group homes or runaway shelters where the most troubled teens gather. Researchers also took at face value the claims that these teens made about their attempts at suicide.

Savin-Williams surveyed a more representative group of teens. He focused on 349 students, ages 17 to 25. When these students told him they had tried to kill themselves, he asked them what method they had used. Savin-Williams discovered the following:

- Over half of these reported suicide attempts turned out to be "thinking about it" rather than attempting it.
- One study of 83 women showed a true suicide rate of 13% for those who hadn't attended a support group. (Between 7% and 13% of all teens have tried to kill themselves, according to latest figures.)
- Another survey of 266 college men and women found that teens who think they are homosexuals were not much more likely to have attempted suicide than straight students. Homosexual students were more likely to have reported "attempts," but these turned out to be "thinking" about suicide rather than actually doing it.

Honest research

According to Savin-Williams, homosexual teen suicide statistics unfairly "pathologize gay youth, and that's not fair to them." Savin-Williams is not "anti-homosexual," but has apparently attempted to conduct honest research.

In fact, Beth Reis, a pro-homosexual activist with the Safe Schools Coalition solicited a clarification from Savin-Williams on his research. Reis was concerned that his work might have been misreported in the media. It was not.

> *Homosexual activists like David Smith have ignored more than a decade of studies debunking the 30% statistic.*

Savin-Williams responded to her by noting: "When I solicit a broad spectrum of youths with same-sex attractions, and not only those who openly identify as gay, lesbian, or bisexual while in high school, and asked in-depth questions about their suicide history, I found statistically no difference in the suicide attempt rate based on sexual attractions. Although same-sex attracted youths initially reported a higher rate of suicide attempts, on further probing this sexual attraction disappeared." Savin-Williams believes that pro-homosexual adults have done a disservice to homosexual teens by creating a "suffering, suicidal, tragic" script for them that often leads these troubled teens to report attempted suicides *when these events did not occur.*

According to Savin-Williams, homosexuals do a disservice to "gay" teens when they "paint them with one rather narrow negative brush stroke." Homosexuals, however, have won great inroads into public schools by claiming that "gay" teens are killing themselves in record numbers. This 30% suicide claim is now gone—and activists are finally being forced to admit this fact—something they had refused to do for more than a decade.

Homosexuals should be kept away from children, not serve as mentors for them in schools.

Human Rights Campaign (HRC), an aggressive homosexual group has continuously pushed the 30% urban legend over the years. HRC spokesman David Smith reluctantly admitted that the 30% figure is wrong, but he told *USA Today*, "Nobody disputes the fact being gay or lesbian in high school is not a very pleasant experience. The core problem is prejudice and harassment that goes unchecked in school settings. School officials take no action. We need to address that problem head-on."

Homosexual activists like David Smith have ignored more than a decade of studies debunking the 30% statistic. As noted above, the 30% urban legend was created by homosexual social worker Paul Gibson in 1989. Gibson's flawed study became an appendix in a Health and Human Services report entitled, "Gay Male and Lesbian Youth Suicide." Although Gibson's work was repudiated by then-Secretary of HHS, Dr. Louis W. Sullivan, homosexual activists were successful in using Gibson's work to push for "gay" counseling programs and "tolerance" curricula in our nation's public schools. Gibson's report, for example, was used by activists in Massachusetts to establish a state-wide gay and lesbian youth commission funded with millions of dollars by the state.

Gibson's 30% figure was based, in part, on a quotation from a homosexual activist in the Washington *Blade* who speculated that 3,000 homosexual teens killed themselves each year.

Inaccurate report still used to promote homosexual agenda

Activists continue to use his report, despite the fact that his work has been debunked. What are the most frequently quoted "facts" from Gibson's report? They are:

1. That homosexual teens account for one third of all teen suicides;
2. That homosexual teens are two to three times more likely to commit suicide than their heterosexual counterparts;
3. That suicide is the leading cause of death among "gay" and "lesbian" youth;
4. That "gay" youth suicide is caused by internalized homophobia and violence directed against struggling teen homosexuals.

Few journalists took the time to actually analyze Gibson's report when it came out. As a result, his non-facts became part of the culture. One enterprising journalist who actually studied the report is Delia M. Rios with the Newhouse News Service. Her report, "Statistics on gay suicides are baseless, researchers say," was published in the *Seattle Times* on May 22, 1997.

Rios quoted Peter Muehrer, with the National Institutes of Mental Health. Muehrer said most major research studies citing a link between sexual orientation and suicide are "limited in both quantity and quality." He also said there are no agreed-upon standards in suicide research and reliable methods for measuring suicide attempts are nonexistent.

> Because of these factors, said Muehrer, ". . . it is not possible to accurately compare suicide attempt rates between gay and lesbian youth and non-gay youth in the general population." According to Muehrer, "There is no scientific evidence to support this (30%) figure."

Peter Labarbera, author of "The Gay Youth Suicide Myth" published by the Family Research Council, quotes Dr. David Shaffer, one of the nation's leading authorities on youth suicide. Shaffer analyzed Gibson's figures and observed: "I struggled for a long time over [Gibson's] mathematics, but, in the end, it seemed more like hocus-pocus than math."

In short, while Gibson's non-facts are still being used by homosexuals to promote the recruitment and seduction of children in our nation's public schools, there is now new evidence from Cornell's Savin-Williams, showing that suicide among homosexual teens is no more likely than among heterosexual teenagers.

The cold, hard fact is that teens who are struggling with homosexual feelings are more likely to be sexually molested by a homosexual school counselor or teacher than to commit suicide over their feelings of despair. In fact, TVC's Special Report, Homosexual Child Molesters reveals new statistics on the high rates of homosexual molestation of children in our nation's public schools. Statistics show that homosexual school personnel account for as many as 40% of all child molestations in schools. The fact that homosexuals account for only 1–2% of the population should be of great concern to parents and school officials. Homosexuals should be kept away from children, not serve as mentors for them in schools.

4

Untreated Teen Depression Can Lead to Suicide

Jim McNulty

Jim McNulty is president of the National Alliance for the Mentally Ill (NAMI), a nonprofit support and advocacy organization of consumers, families, and friends of people with severe mental illnesses.

The symptoms of mental illness in children that often lead to suicide have long been ignored in the United States. In America, one in ten children and adolescents have a mental illness severe enough to cause impairment. A national response to this crisis, including screening, treatment, and services for children suffering from depression and other mental illnesses, must be funded in order to reduce teen suicide.

Editor's Note: The following viewpoint was originally given as testimony before the Senate Health, Education, Labor, and Pensions Subcommittee on Children and Families.

The United States Surgeon General has reported that every year, more man 30,000 Americans take their own lives. Suicide is the eighth-leading cause of death in the United States, and the third among our youth, ages 15 to 24. Most suffer from treatable mental illnesses, biological-based brain disorders that can lead to tragic consequences. The majority suffers from some form of depression. NAMI has long been concerned with the issue of suicide among children and adolescents and applauds this Subcommittee for bringing attention to this issue.

What is NAMI?

NAMI, the National Alliance for the Mentally Ill, is the leading family member and consumer grassroots membership organization in the nation dedicated to improving the lives of individuals with severe mental illnesses and their family members. NAMI was founded in Madison, Wis-

Jim McNulty, testimony before the Subcommittee on Children and Families, Senate Committee on Health, Education, Labor, and Pensions, Washington, DC, 2001.

consin in 1979 and currently has over 220,000 members, 50 state organizations and over 1,200 local affiliates. Through these chapters and affiliates in all 50 states, NAMI supports education, outreach, advocacy and research on behalf of persons with serious brain disorders such as schizophrenia, manic depressive illness, major depression, severe anxiety disorders and major mental illnesses affecting children.

The pressing need for action

For too long, the needs of children and adolescents experiencing symptoms of mental illnesses and the links to teen suicide have been ignored. United States Surgeon General David Satcher, M.D., Ph.D., released a report on children's mental health in January 2001 that soundly identifies the public health crisis caused by our nation's failure to recognize and treat childhood mental illnesses.

The Surgeon General's Conference on Children's Mental Health: A National Action Agenda, found that in the United States, 1 in 10 children and adolescents have a mental illness severe enough to cause impairment. However in any given year, fewer than 1 in 5 of these children receives needed treatment. According to recent evidence compiled by the World Health Organization, by the year 2020, childhood neuropsychiatric disorders will rise proportionately by over 50 percent, internationally, to become one of the five most common causes of childhood morbidity, mortality, and disability.

Suicide is the eighth-leading cause of death in the United States, and the third among our youth, ages 15 to 24.

Families with children are suffering because of missed opportunities for early identification and the fragmentation of treatment services. NAMI strongly supports many of the identified goals and action steps of the Surgeon General's National Action Agenda for Children's Mental Health that include:

- Promote public awareness of children and adolescents and reduce the stigma associated with mental illness.
- Continue to develop, disseminate, and implement scientifically-proven treatment and early intervention services in the field of children's mental health.
- Improve the assessment and recognition of mental illness in children and adolescents.
- Eliminate racial/ethnic and socioeconomic disparities in access to mental illness treatment.
- Improve the infrastructure for children's mental health services including support for scientifically-proven interventions across professions.
- Increase access to and coordination of quality mental healthcare services.
- Train frontline providers to recognize and manage mental health

issues, and educate mental health providers in scientifically-proven treatment services.

• Monitor the access to and coordination of quality mental illness treatment services.

Child and adolescent suicide: a national tragedy

The American Psychiatric Association (APA) reports that suicide is the second leading cause of death among young people ages 15 to 19 years and that every day, 14 young people (ages 15 to 24) commit suicide, or approximately 1 every 100 minutes. The APA has also found that most people who commit suicide have a diagnosable mental illness or substance abuse disorder and that fifty-three percent of young people that take their own lives are abusing substances and the majority have co-occurring disorders.

Families with children are suffering because of missed opportunities for early identification and the fragmentation of treatment services.

Although the evidence supporting the crisis of teen suicide is clear, the lack of available and accessible treatment is a major concern. The Surgeon General reports that there is substantial evidence that the nation lacks a unified infrastructure to help these children and many are falling through the cracks. Many NAMI families are aware that, too often, children who are not identified as having mental health problems and who do not receive services end up in the juvenile justice system. Within this system, recent studies have found that fifteen percent of all youth mandated or incarcerated in "boot camps" have a serious mental illness such as bipolar or schizophrenia. Another recently published report indicates that fifty to seventy-five percent of children in juvenile justice institutions are youngsters of color who have never had access to mental health screening or treatment.

Lack of coordinated systems of care

NAMI documented this public crisis in a 1999 report that identified systems of mental health care created to address the needs of children and adolescents, and how these systems are failing the children they are meant to serve. This report, Families on the Brink, explains how this lack of care results in potential lasting harm to the affected children and their families and in broad dissatisfaction with treatment options and capacity. As the executive summary points out, "The overall picture is one of major barriers to care, with devastating results for the children and the families. . . . In more than half the families, fifty-five percent, one of the parents had to change jobs or quit to take care of their ailing offspring. Fifty-nine percent said they felt like they were pushed to the breaking point." Most alarmingly the Families on the Brink report found that twenty-three percent of surveyed parents had been counseled or advised to a counselor relinquishing custody to the state in order to ensure eligibility for care or residential services.

A congressional response needed

Mr. Chairman, NAMI recommends that this Committee and Congress take the following steps to address this public health crisis:

1. Fully fund the suicide prevention initiative that was authorized by Congress in the Children's Health Act of 2000 (section 3111 of PL 106-310). This important new program calls on SAMHSA [Substance Abuse and Mental Health Services Administration], NIMH [National Institute of Mental Health], CDC [Centers for Disease Control and Prevention], HRSA [Health Resources and Services Administration], and ACF [Administration for Children and Families] to support evidence-based suicide prevention programs. These include timely assessment and treatment for children and adolescents most at risk for suicide and increased integration of suicide prevention strategies with other systems such as education and juvenile justice. NAMI strongly urges Congress to appropriate the full $75 million for this program in FY 2002.

2. Create new incentives for states and communities to invest in evidence-based screening and assessment tools for children and adolescents with mental illness. The most promising of these evidence-based tools is the Diagnostic Interview Schedule for Children (DISC). The DISC was developed in 1979 at the National Institute of Mental Health and is a comprehensive interview that covers 36 mental health disorders for children and adolescents, using DSM-IV criteria. This evidence-based model can be self-administered using computerized voice files and produces a series of diagnostic reports. This tool can work in conjunction with school-based educational programs that attempt to provide early identification and assessment. Further, it can reduce the stigma of mental illnesses and suicide and teach about mental illness including the risk factors and symptoms.

3. NAMI strongly supports passage of the Family Opportunity Act (S 321/HR 600). This legislation, introduced by Senators Chuck Grassley (R-IA) and Edward Kennedy (D-MA) and Representatives Pete Sessions (R-TX) and Henry Waxman (D-CA), is intended to restore hope for children with severe mental illnesses and their families. The Family Opportunity Act would allow states to set up Medicaid buy-in programs for children with severe disabilities so that parents would not be forced to relinquish custody of their children or declare bankruptcy to get coverage for the treatment their child needs. S 321/HR 600 would also establish "Family to Family Health Information Centers" which would assist and support families of children with disabilities and/or special health care needs. These centers, staffed by both parents of children with special needs and professionals, would provide technical assistance and information to families on health care programs and services available and appropriate for children with disabilities and/or special needs.

4. Congress should renew The Better Pharmaceuticals for Children

Act (S 838) that will expire later this year. This bill will amend the Federal Food, Drug and Cosmetic Act to improve the safety and efficacy of pharmaceuticals for children. Congress should encourage NIMH and private industry funding of basic scientific research on effective interventions that can reduce the risk of suicide among children and adolescents. While there is ample evidence on effective screening and prevention strategies, there is still little understanding on the effects of treatment on at-risk populations. Conducting scientific research and testing new medications to treat severe mental illness for children and adolescents is critical.

5. In addition NAMI urges Congress to continue its bipartisan effort to double the budget of the NIH by 2004 to ensure that there are adequate resources for this research.

6. Congress should pass S 543, the Mental Health Equitable Treatment Act of 2001. NAMI greatly appreciates the work of this Committee in favorably reporting out this important legislation on August 1. The risk of suicide will continue to be increased so long as health plans offer discriminatory coverage for the treatment they need. Parity will ensure greater access to the treatment that can save the lives of those most at risk.

Conclusion

This hearing along with the Surgeon General's report has generated long overdue attention to the remarkable absence of appropriate screening, treatment and services for children and adolescents with mental illnesses. Local and national media continue to feature reports and articles confirming the crisis our children face as a result of the failure of a fragmented mental health system.

5

Teens Who Are Teased About Their Weight Are More Likely to Commit Suicide

Daniel J. DeNoon

Daniel J. DeNoon is a senior medical writer for WebMD, a Web site featuring daily news stories and health information.

Since teens are sensitive about their appearance, youths who are teased about their weight often suffer from low self-esteem and other depressive symptoms, and they are at much higher risk of suicide. Today, obesity is epidemic among Americans of all ages, including teens. Parents should teach their children that the ideal body is not extremely thin or extremely muscular and make sure no teasing occurs at home. Moreover, parents should find out if their child is being teased at school, and if so, they should contact the parent of the teaser.

Suicide and other emotional health problems haunt teens who are teased about their weight. And it's not just overweight kids who suffer.

A new study finds that kids who get teased about their weight are two to three times as likely to think about suicide or actually try to kill themselves. Weight teasing has this destructive effect on all teens—not just those who are overweight.

Teens are very sensitive to how they look. Obesity is epidemic among Americans of all ages. Yet our cultural ideals for both men and women are getting thinner and more buff than ever, notes study leader Marla E. Eisenberg, ScD, MPH, of the University of Minnesota, Minneapolis. Teens are particularly sensitive about how they look to their peers.

"We are living in a society where we are constantly being bombarded with images of the perfect body," Eisenberg tells WebMD. "Marketing links perfect bodies to happiness and beauty and romance. When teens look at their own bodies—even if they're healthy—they come up short and think they are not good people and won't get all the good things that should be coming to them."

This makes them enormously vulnerable to emotional wounds from teasing, says Nancy Cahir, PhD, an Atlanta-based clinical psychologist who works with families and children.

"Teasing about weight in this day and age—when kids are so obsessed with self-image—is a low blow," Cahir tells WebMD.

A little teasing hurts a lot

Eisenberg's findings bear out Cahir's clinical impression. Her team had nearly 5,000 kids in grades 7 to 12 fill out a questionnaire during school hours. They found that 30% of girls and 25% of boys got teased about their weight by their peers. Sadly, 29% of girls and 16% of boys got teased by their families. About 15% of the girls and 10% of the boys were teased by both peers and their families.

Teasing took its toll. Kids who got teased about their weight hated their bodies. They had low self-esteem and other depressive symptoms. And most frighteningly, weight-teased teens were at much higher risk of suicide.

"Being teased is a profound experience for these kids," Eisenberg says. "A really important finding was [that] the experience of being teased was important above and beyond teens' actual body weight."

Teens are particularly sensitive about how they look to their peers.

The findings appear in the August issue of *Archives of Pediatrics & Adolescent Medicine*.

Cahir says just a little teasing comes to hurt a lot.

"Teasing is insidious. It usually happens over time," she says. "Every day the teen gets a comment that embeds in the psyche more and more—they start brewing. The teens feel so rejected and think they can't say anything. That is the part that causes the most damage."

The study found that teasing by family members was particularly harmful—even if it wasn't meant to hurt.

"Your parents hold a lot of your emotional needs for love and affection and validation you are OK. So if they don't give it—but tease instead—it hurts that much more," Cahir says. "And the worst damage is done by family members. It is just brutal. When it comes from the people who know them the most—who are supposed to love them the most—it hurts the most."

Take action, not revenge

What can you do to protect your teen against teasing? Start at home, Eisenberg advises.

"The really important first step is to raise awareness of what kind of comments a teen considers hurtful," she says. "Parents really can cut out the teasing. If they have legitimate concerns about a child's weight problem, there are kinder and gentler ways to approach that."

Don't further stigmatize overweight teens by singling them out for restrictions.

"Parents can say, 'Your body isn't healthy—so we as a family need to change our nutrition and exercise habits,'" she says. "When change is taken on as a family event—not as a way to be punitive, not as a matter of deprivation—it can work. Say, 'We are going to have more healthy foods around. We are going to make some changes in our family activities that will help you get in a healthier body.'"

Eisenberg also urges parents to teach children that the ideal body isn't extremely thin or extremely muscular.

"Your body is good if it works properly, not if it looks like some ideal," she says. "The ideal must change from being beautiful to being well."

Cahir also has some tips for dealing with weight teasing:

- Don't respond to teasing with violence. Some parents tell their kids to fight. That's wrong, she says. Teens have to learn to use words to resolve conflicts. Tell the teasers you want them to stop—and if they don't, you'll report them to school officials.
- Sometimes children may be inciting teasing without knowing it. It might be that they say provocative things, or dress oddly. Gently suggest other ways of acting or dressing. If the child's clothing is clearly inappropriate, insist on different dress.
- Talk to your kids about their day. Ask whether they got teased today. If you know another kid often teases them, you can ask if they saw that child today.
- If a brother or sister is teasing a child, tell the teaser that this isn't how we act in our family. The teaser needs to be told to apologize. Explore why the teasing is happening. If the teaser is angry, talk about what the anger is about. Don't just say, "Stop it." Use the teasing behavior as a springboard for family communication. That child who is teasing has some issues going on as well.
- It might be helpful to contact the parent of teaser, if it's not done in hostile way. Say, "Sammy is teasing Johnny. Any idea what that is about? Is teasing done in your family?" Often the worst teasers are getting it at home themselves.

Stop suicide

Parents can do a lot to prevent teen suicide. The most important thing, Cahir says, is to keep in touch with your children and their moods.

"If teens spend a lot of time alone, don't assume it is growing pains and hormones," she advises. "Make sure your child is talking with you. Lots of time spent alone is a symptom. Others are not having friends over, or not wanting to be with friends. Look for comments about self-esteem, statements like, 'Other kids don't seem to like me.'"

If your child is becoming isolated, be safe. Get a referral to a child or family psychologist or psychiatrist.

6

Sexually Active Teens Are More Likely to Commit Suicide

Robert E. Rector, Kirk A. Johnson, and Lauren R. Noyes

Robert E. Rector is a senior research fellow, Kirk A. Johnson is Harry and Jeanette Weinberg Fellow in Statistical Welfare Research in the Center for Data Analysis, and Lauren R. Noyes is director of Research Projects in Domestic Policy at the Heritage Foundation, a public policy research institute.

Studies show a strong correlation between teenage sexual activity and suicide rates. Sexually active teenage girls are three times as likely to attempt suicide as teenage girls who are not sexually active, while sexually active teenage boys are eight times as likely to attempt suicide as teenage boys who are not sexually active. These figures remain roughly consistent across racial, ethnic, and socio-economic categories. Youths who are sexually active report being unhappy in greater numbers than teens who are not sexually active. Consequently, safe-sex education programs in schools should be replaced by abstinence education programs, which will better protect the physical and mental health of teenagers.

Teenage sexual activity is an issue of widespread national concern. Although teen sexual activity has declined in recent years, the overall rate is still high. In 1997, approximately 48 percent of American teenagers of high-school age were or had been sexually active.

The problems associated with teen sexual activity are well-known. Every day, 8,000 teenagers in the United become infected by a sexually transmitted disease. This year, nearly 3 million teens will become infected. Overall, roughly one-quarter of the nation's sexually active teens have been infected by a sexually transmitted disease (STD).

The problems of pregnancy and out-of-wedlock childbearing are also severe. In 2000, some 240,000 children were born to girls aged 18 or younger. Nearly all these teenage mothers were unmarried. These mothers and their children have an extremely high probability of long-term poverty and welfare dependence. Less widely known are the psychological and emotional problems associated with teenage sexual activity. The present study examines the linkage between teenage sexual activity and emotional health. The findings show that:

> When compared to teens who are not sexually active, teenage boys and girls who are sexually active are significantly less likely to be happy and more likely to feel depressed.

> When compared to teens who are not sexually active, teenage boys and girls who are sexually active are significantly more likely to attempt suicide.

Thus, in addition to its role in promoting teen pregnancy and the current epidemic of STDs, early sexual activity is a substantial factor in undermining the emotional well-being of American teenagers.

Data source and methods

The data used in this analysis are taken from the National Longitudinal Survey of Adolescent Health, Wave II, 1996. This "Ad-Health" survey is a nationwide survey designed to examine the health-related behaviors of adolescents in middle school and high school. Its public-use database contains responses from approximately 6,500 adolescents, representative of teenagers across the nation. The survey is funded by the National Institute of Child Health and Human Development (NICHD) and 17 other federal agencies.

This Heritage CDA analysis focuses on the link between sexual activity and emotional well-being among teens in high school years (ages 14 through 17). The Ad-Health survey asks students whether they have "ever had sexual intercourse." For purposes of analysis, teens who answered yes to this question are labeled as "sexually active" and those who answered no are labeled as "not sexually active."

A full 14.3 percent of girls who are sexually active report having attempted suicide. By contrast, only 5.1 percent of sexually inactive girls have attempted suicide.

The survey also records the emotional health of teens. Students are asked how often, in the past week, they "felt depressed." They are provided with four possible answers to the question: They felt depressed

(a) Never or rarely,
(b) Sometimes,
(c) A lot of the time, or
(d) Most of the time or all of the time.

For purposes of analysis, the classification of depressed is given to those teens who answered yes to options "c" or "d"—that is, they said they felt depressed a lot, most, or all of the time. Thus, throughout the paper, the terms "depressed" or "depression" refer to this general state of continuing unhappiness rather than to a more specific sense of clinical depression.

Sexual activity and depression

The Ad-Health data reveal substantial differences in emotional health between those teens who are sexually active and those who are not:

> A full quarter (25.3 percent) of teenage girls who are sexually active report that they are depressed all, most, or a lot of the time. By contrast, only 7.7 percent of teenage girls who are not sexually active report that they are depressed all, most, or a lot of the time. Thus, sexually active girls are more than three times more likely to be depressed than are girls who are not sexually active.

> Some 8.3 percent of teenage boys who are sexually active report that they are depressed all, most, or a lot of the time. By contrast, only 3.4 percent of teenage boys who are not sexually active are depressed all, most, or a lot of the time. Thus, boys who are sexually active are more than twice as likely to be depressed as are those who are not sexually active.

A full 60.2 percent of sexually inactive girls report that they "rarely or never" feel depressed. For sexually active teen girls, the number is far lower: only 36.8 percent. Overall, for either gender, teens who are not sexually active are markedly happier than those who are active.

Among boys, 6.0 percent of those who are sexually active have attempted suicide. By contrast, only 0.7 percent of boys who are not sexually active have attempted suicide.

The link between teen sexual activity and depression is supported by clinical experience. Doctor of adolescent medicine Meg Meeker writes, "Teenage sexual activity routinely leads to emotional turmoil and psychological distress. . . . [Sexual permissiveness leads] to empty relationships, to feelings of self-contempt and worthlessness. All, of course, precursors to depression."

Sexual activity and attempted suicide

The Ad-Health survey also asks students whether they have attempted suicide during the past year. The link between sexual activity and attempted suicide is clear.

A full 14.3 percent of girls who are sexually active report having attempted suicide. By contrast, only 5.1 percent of sexually inactive girls have attempted suicide. Thus, sexually active girls are nearly three times more likely to attempt suicide than are girls who are not sexually active.

Among boys, 6.0 percent of those who are sexually active have attempted suicide. By contrast, only 0.7 percent of boys who are not sexually active have attempted suicide. Thus, sexually active teenage boys are eight times more likely to attempt suicide than are boys who are not sexually active.

Social factors

The differences in emotional health between sexually active and inactive teens are clear. However, it is possible that the differences in emotional well-being might be driven by social background factors rather than sexual activity *per se*. For example, if students of lower socioeconomic status are more likely to be sexually active, the greater frequency of depression among those teens might be caused by socioeconomic status rather than sexual activity.

To account for that possibility, additional analysis was performed in which race, gender, exact age, and family income were entered as control variables. This means that each teen was compared to other teens who were identical in gender, age, race, and income.

The introduction of these control or background variables had virtually no effect on the correlations between sexual activity and depression and suicide. In simple terms, when teens were compared to other teens who were identical in gender, race, age, and family income, those who were sexually active were significantly more likely to be depressed and to attempt suicide than were those who were not sexually active.

Teens express regrets over sexual activity

The significantly lower levels of happiness and higher levels of depression among sexually active teens suggest that sexual activity leads to a decrease in happiness and well-being among many, if not most, teenagers. This conclusion is corroborated by the fact that the majority of sexually active teens express reservations and concerns about their personal sexual activity.

For example, a recent poll by the National Campaign to Prevent Teen Pregnancy asked the question, "If you have had sexual intercourse, do you wish you had waited longer?" Among those teens who reported that they had engaged in intercourse, nearly two-thirds stated that they wished they had waited longer before becoming sexually active. By contrast, only one-third of sexually active teens asserted that their commencement of sexual activity was appropriate and that they did not wish they had waited until they were older. Thus, among sexually active teens, those who regretted early sexual activity outnumbered those without such concerns by nearly two to one.

Concerns and regrets about sexual activity are strongest among teenage girls. Almost three-quarters of sexually active teen girls admit they wish they had delayed sexual activity until they were older. Among sexually active teenage girls, those with regrets concerning their initial sexual activity outnumbered those without regrets by nearly three to one.

The dissatisfaction and regrets expressed by teenagers concerning their own sexual activity is striking. Overall, a majority of sexually active boys and nearly three-quarters of sexually active girls regard their own initial sexual experience unfavorably—as an event they wish they had avoided.

Different interpretations

While the association between teen sexual activity and depression is clear, that association may be subject to different theoretical interpretations. For example, it might be that depressed teenagers turn to sexual activity in an effort to assuage or escape their depression. In this interpretation, the link between sexual activity and depression might be caused by a higher level of sexual activity among those who are already depressed before commencing sexual activity. Thus, depression might lead to greater sexual activity rather than sexual activity's leading to depression.

Overall, a majority of sexually active boys and nearly three-quarters of sexually active girls regard their own initial sexual experience unfavorably—as an event they wish they had avoided.

In limited cases, this explanation may be correct; some depressed teens may experiment with sexual activity in an effort to escape their depression. However, as a general interpretation of the linkage between depression and teen sexual activity, this reasoning seems inadequate for two reasons. First, the differences in happiness and depression between sexually active and inactive teens are widespread and are not the result of a small number of depressed individuals. This is especially true for girls. Second, the fact that a majority of teens express regrets concerning their own initial sexual activity strongly suggests that such activity leads to distress and emotional turmoil among many, if not most, teens.

Hence, the most likely explanation of the overall link between teen sexual activity and depression is that early sexual activity leads to emotional stress and reduces teen happiness.

Moreover, theoretical questions about whether teen sexual activity leads to depression or, conversely, whether depression leads to teen sexual activity should not distract attention from the clear message that adult society should be sending to teens. Teens should be told that sexual activity in teen years is clearly linked to reduced personal happiness. Teens who are depressed should be informed that sexual activity is likely to exacerbate, rather than alleviate, their depression. Teens who are not depressed should be told that sexual activity in teen years is likely to substantially reduce their happiness and personal well-being.

Abstinence education programs

Sexual activity among teenagers is the major driving factor behind the well-publicized problems of the high incidence of teenage STDs and teen pregnancy. The analysis presented in this paper also shows that sexual activity is directly connected to substantial problems among teens regarding emotional health.

Teenagers of both genders who are sexually active are substantially less likely to be happy and more likely to be depressed than are teenagers who are not sexually active.

Teenagers of both genders who are sexually active are substantially more likely to attempt suicide than are teenagers who are not sexually active.

Until recently, society provided teenagers with classroom instruction in "safe sex" and "comprehensive sex education." In general, these curricula fail to provide a strong message to delay sexual activity, fail to deal adequately with the long-term emotional and moral aspects of sexuality, and fail to provide students with the skills needed to develop intimate loving marital relationships as adults.

Over the past five years, there has been a growth in abstinence education programs that stand in sharp contrast to "safe sex" curricula. The best abstinence education programs teach:

- The primary importance of delaying sexual activity,
- That human sexual relationships are predominantly emotional and moral rather than physical in character, and
- That teen abstinence is an important step leading toward a loving marital relationship as an adult.

Such abstinence education programs are uniquely suited to meeting both the emotional and the physical needs of America's youth.

7

Teen Bullies and Their Victims Are More Likely to Commit Suicide

Riittakerttu Kaltiala-Heino, Matti Rimpelä, Mauri Marttunen, Arja Rimpelä, and Päivi Rantanen

Riittakerttu Kaltiala-Heino is a senior assistant professor at the University of Tampere in Helsinki, Finland. Matti Rimpelä is a professor at the National Research and Development Centre for Welfare and Health in Helsinki. Mauri Marttunen is a senior researcher at the Department of Mental Health and Alcohol Research at the National Public Health Institute in Helsinki. Arja Rimpelä is a professor at the Department of Adolescent Psychiatry at the University of Tampere. Päivi Rantanen is a professor at the Tampere University Hospital.

Studies indicate that bullying and being bullied lead to stress and depression. Indeed, research indicates that there is an increased prevalence of depression and suicidal ideation among both teens who are bullied and teens who are bullies. Suicidal thoughts are most common among those students who have been both bullied by others and who are also bullies themselves. The need for psychiatric intervention should be considered not only for victims of bullying but also for bullies themselves.

About 1 in 10 schoolchildren report being bullied weekly at school. Boys are involved in bullying, both as victims and as bullies, more often than girls. Primary school children are more likely to be victims of bullying than adolescents, but the number of bullies tends to remain constant between primary school and secondary school.

The possible association between being bullied and the risk of suicide has been recognised by adolescent psychiatrists, but epidemiological studies have not assessed the correlation. [G.] Salmon et al found an association between being bullied and being depressed. In children, being bullied has been associated with an increase in psychological and psychosomatic symptoms. [K.] Williams et al found that children who were frequently bullied at school were more likely to wet their beds, have difficulty sleeping, and have headaches and abdominal pain. [K.] Kumpulainen et al found an association between involvement in bullying (being bullied or being a bully) and a number of behavioural and psychological symptoms including depression in children in primary school. Anxiety, a fear of going to school, feelings of being unsafe and unhappy at school, and low self esteem have all been reported to be consequences of repeatedly being bullied. Depression has also been linked to being bullied.

Being a bully in childhood and adolescence has been associated with delinquency in adulthood. Being bullied has been associated with poorer perceived health, depression, and with mental disorders in adulthood.

The aim of this study was to investigate the association between bullying, depression, and severe suicidal ideation among adolescents aged 14–16 in Finland.

Participants and methods

The school health promotion study is a classroom survey focusing on adolescent health, health behaviour, and behaviour in school; it has been carried out annually in Finland every April since 1995. The health promotion study has been approved by the ethical committee of Tampere University Hospital.

In 1997, students in the 8th and 9th grades of secondary school (ages 14–16 years) in two regions in Finland (Vaasa and Pirkanmaa) participated in the study. Out of a total of 20 213 pupils in these schools, 2570 (13%) were absent on the day of the survey. Altogether, 17 643 pupils (87%) returned the questionnaire (8695 girls, 8948 boys). A total of 1179 students (6.7%) gave incomplete responses on the Beck inventory and their questionnaires were excluded from the analysis. An additional 54 respondents did not answer the questions about bullying and were also excluded from the analysis. We were thus able to analyse the responses of 16 410 students (81% of the target population, 93% of those present at school).

Depression and severe suicidal ideation were more common among those respondents who were being bullied or who were bullies.

Involvement in bullying either as a bully or as the person being bullied was evaluated using two questions derived from a World Health Organisation study on youth health. The subject was introduced as follows:

The next questions are about bullying. We say a pupil is being bullied when another pupil, or a group of pupils, says or does nasty and unpleasant things to him or her. It is also bullying when a pupil is teased repeatedly in a way he or she doesn't like. But it is not bullying when two pupils of about the same strength quarrel or fight.

The students were asked how frequently they had been bullied during the current school term (from the beginning of January until the end of May) and how frequently they had bullied others. They were asked to indicate whether these actions had occurred many times a week, about once a week, less frequently, or not at all. Those who bullied others at least once a week were classed as frequently being bullies; those who were bullied at least once a week were classed as frequently being bullied. Respondents were classed as not participating in bullying or being bullied, as being bullied or being a bully less than weekly, as frequently acting as a bully and not being bullied, as frequently being bullied and not a bully, or as frequently being both bullied and a bully.

After adjusting for age and sex, the highest risk of severe suicidal ideation was seen among students who were both bullied and were also bullies.

Depression was measured using a modified, 13 item version of the Beck depression inventory which had been validated in Finnish. The Beck inventory has been shown to be a valid measure for detecting depression among adolescents. It has good psychometric properties in this population. Students who scored from 0 to 7 were classed as having no depression or mild depression, and those who had scores of 8 to 39 were classed as having moderate to severe depression.

One of the items on the inventory asks about thoughts of self harm. We classed the students as having severe suicidal ideation if they chose either "I have definite plans about committing suicide" or "I would kill myself if I had the chance."

The sociodemographic variables evaluated were age, sex, years since moving to current area, educational level attained by parents, whether one or both parents had been unemployed during the past 12 months, and family structure (whether the adolescent was living with both parents, with one parent, with a step-parent, or apart from the parents). School performance was measured using the child's grade point average; perceived lack of social support from parents, friends, and teachers were used as independent variables. Grade point average and perceived social support have been shown to be determinants of depression in the sample studied. . . .

Results

Five per cent (373/8196) of the girls and 6% (464/8214) of the boys had been bullied weekly during the current school term. Two per cent (196/8196) of the girls and 9% (705/8214) of the boys reported that they had bullied others at least weekly.

Eleven per cent (915/8196) of the girls and 6% (508/8214) of the boys were classed as being moderately to severely depressed. Severe suicidal ideation was reported by 2% (197/8196) of girls and 2% (170/8214) of boys.

Depression and severe suicidal ideation were more common among those respondents who were being bullied or who were bullies. Depression occurred equally frequently among those who were bullied and those who were bullies, and it was most common among those who were both bullied by others and were also bullies themselves. Among girls, severe suicidal ideation was associated with frequently being bullied or being a bully, and for boys it was associated with being a bully. . . .

After adjusting for age and sex, the highest risk of depression was seen among those students who were both bullied and were also bullies (odds ratio 9.4); the next highest risk was seen among those who were bullied (odds ratio 5.1). The odds ratio among bullies was 4.5. Fitting other demographic and social variables that correlate with depression into the model confirmed the association.

Involvement in bullying persisted as a risk for severe suicidal ideation in the multivariate analysis. After adjusting for age and sex, the highest risk of severe suicidal ideation was seen among students who were both bullied and were also bullies (odds ratio 12.1). The next highest risk was among those who were bullies (odds ratio 8.7). The odds ratio for those who were bullied was 5.7. When depressive symptoms were added to the analysis, the highest risk of severe suicidal ideation was, however, seen among those who were bullies (odds ratio 4.4); the next highest risk was among those who were both bullied and were also bullies (odds ratio 3.1). The odds ratio for those who were bullied was 2.5. After other determinants of depression were added to the final model, the greatest risk of severe suicidal ideation was detected among bullies, followed by those who were both bullied and were also bullies, and then by those who were bullied.

This study provides a good opportunity to assess cross sectional relations between being bullied or being a bully, self reported depression, and severe suicidal ideation. The sample is large and representative of the mid-adolescent population in Finland. More than 99% of children and adolescents aged 7 to 16 attend primary and secondary school. The participation rate for the survey was high. However, psychological problems, depression, and experiences of being a bully or being bullied may be more common among those pupils who were absent. Therefore, the prevalences of bullying, depression, and severe suicidal ideation detected in this study are likely to be underestimates.

The 13 item Beck inventory measures the respondent's own perception of her or his depressive symptoms but it is not a diagnostic instrument for depressive disorders. Because the inventory measures a psychological state we could not assess the duration of depressive symptoms. However, severe depressive symptoms in adolescents are likely to be comparatively persistent. . . .

Transient death wishes and non-specific suicidal ideation have been reported to be comparatively common during adolescence. Therefore, only responses indicating severe suicidal ideation with an intent were included in the analyses.

Bullying and mental health

Depression and severe suicidal ideation are strongly linked to being bullied or to acting as a bully. Even an infrequent involvement in bullying (being bullied or being a bully) increases the likelihood of severe suicidal ideation, independent of depression.

Being bullied frequently is likely to be a considerable source of stress. Depression among those who were frequently bullied might be expected. However, adolescents who are depressed may also attract negative attention from their peers. Previous research suggests that compared with their peers, those who are bullied are more introverted, less assertive, and are overinvolved in their families. Victims also tend to be rejected by peers. Depression could thus be both a result of and a reason for being bullied. A longitudinal design is necessary to study causality. However, in this study severe suicidal ideation was increased among those who were bullied regardless of whether they were depressed. This emphasises the stressful nature of being bullied and highlights the importance of taking action to stop bullying.

> *Teachers and clinicians should recognise that being bullied or being a bully are signs of an increased risk of depression and suicidal behaviour among adolescents.*

Although the association between being a bully and depression has not received attention in previous research, bullies have been shown to have certain mental health problems. Being a bully has been associated with juvenile delinquency, alcohol misuse, violence in adulthood, and criminal behaviour. The social background of bullies also suggests that they are vulnerable to psychiatric morbidity. Being a bully has been associated with rejection by peers and social isolation. In bullies' families, more emotional distance between family members, a lack of warmth, and inconsistent discipline for children has been noted. Bullies thus need support for normal development to proceed, and any interventions should also recognise the role of depressive disorders in the background of their behaviour.

The role of the adolescent remains constant in the long process of being bullied or being a bully. The strong association between being a bully or being bullied, depression, and severe suicidal ideation highlights the importance of further investigations into the social, psychological, and environmental factors associated with bullying.

Intervention

Teachers and clinicians should recognise that being bullied or being a bully are signs of an increased risk of depression and suicidal behaviour among adolescents. Adolescents should be asked if they are involved in bullying either as a victim or as a bully. Whether an intervention is needed to treat depression should be assessed among both bullies and those who are being bullied. A cross disciplinary approach is needed to identify effective interventions to prevent bullying and depression and to reduce the risk of suicide while keeping in mind the close association between these phenomena.

8

Stricter Gun Control Would Reduce Teen Suicide

Chris Mooney

Chris Mooney is an American Prospect *contributing writer. He has contributed to a variety of other publications as well, including* Lingua Franca, Slate, Salon, American Scholar, Washington Monthly, *the* Washington Post, *and the* Boston Globe.

In any given year, more than half of all U.S. gun-related deaths are suicides, not, as is commonly believed, homicides. A connection exists between gun availability and risk of suicide, especially among youth. Unfortunately, government has been unable to restrict access to guns because of the influence of the gun lobby, particularly the National Rifle Association (NRA). In order to begin reducing the number of suicides committed using firearms, the NRA must acknowledge that a gun in the home often leads to tragedy.

It was Sunday morning, Mother's Day. In Washington, D.C., the Clintons were welcoming Million Mom Marchers at the White House before their rally, while near the Washington Monument, the Second Amendment Sisters were beginning to assemble. But in North Michigan, in the town of Menominee near the Wisconsin border, it was also the morning after the local high school's prom, and B.J. Stupak, son of the four-term Democratic Congressman Bart Stupak, had been found dead in his home. The apparently thriving high school junior—recently elected president of the student council and named to prom court—had shot himself.

As Capitol Hill mourned the tragic death of Stupak's son, Republican Congresswoman Mary Bono decided something had to be done. She sent an open letter to the National Rifle Association's Wayne LaPierre, encouraging the group "to inform parents, teens and all gun owners of the potentially dangerous connection between the access to a gun and suicide." In B.J.'s case, the connection was lethal: According to police reports, the gun he used belonged to a family member.

There was painful irony to B.J. Stupak's death, in that his father is a member of the most visible organization promoting gun ownership; Stupak is one of Congress's few "NRA Democrats." A former police officer and state trooper, [in 1999] Bart Stupak said in an interview, "I'm a member of the NRA, my wife's a member of the NRA, our sons are members of the NRA."

Mary Bono's chief of staff Frank Cullen insists that "in no way was Congresswoman Bono attempting to characterize the incident" of B.J.'s death, or to speak for the Stupak family. Whatever the case, it was a rare, and slightly edgy moment: a Republican mother goading the NRA, while a Democratic father swallowed his grief.

The crisis

Since the shootings at Columbine high school in April of 1999, stories of kids murdering kids have dominated gun control debates. But B.J. Stupak's death draws attention to an astonishing, but rarely cited figure: In any given year, more than half of all U.S. gun-related deaths are not homicides at all, but suicides.

According to some, this little known fact could help reshape the gun issue. Today, the NRA insists that the only way for responsible Americans to protect their families from criminals is to own a gun—and countless families have acted on that warning. But what the organization fails to tell its members and others is that in most gun deaths, the shooter is also the victim.

"If you really want to understand the issue of benefits and costs of firearms, you have to know what's happening with suicides," says David Hemenway, director of the Harvard Injury Control Research Center. What's happening is this: Suicide is the eighth leading cause of death in the U.S., and more Americans commit suicide using guns than with all other means combined. On average, 50 people kill themselves with guns every day.

In 1997, there were almost 18,000 gun suicides, compared to roughly 13,000 gun homicides. (This is the last year for which statistics are currently available.) In some states, the gun suicide to homicide ratio is actually far higher: In Colorado, for example, it is three to one.

Since many suicide attempts are the result of impulsive behavior, this means access to a gun can easily turn a passing bout of depression into a tragedy.

Guns are also the most deadly weapon used in suicide attempts; guns kill more than nine out of 10 people who attempt suicide with them, according to one study. Since many suicide attempts are the result of impulsive behavior, this means access to a gun can easily turn a passing bout of depression into a tragedy. "If they didn't have [a gun] handy, they might try suicide by other means, but they'd be more likely to survive and get counseling," says Kristen Rand, federal affairs director at the Violence Policy Center.

But perhaps most significantly—and as Mary Bono's letter to the NRA pointed out—there appears to be a connection between gun availibility and risk of suicide, especially among youth. A number of studies, including several in the *New England Journal of Medicine*, have confirmed this link. According to the federal Centers for Disease Control and Prevention (CDC), "people living in households in which guns are kept have a risk of suicide that is five times greater than people living in households without guns."

Government's silence

Despite these horrifying statistics, those in the federal government have only recently begun to talk about suicide—and they have almost completely ignored the gun connection. Indeed, although Senators Edward Kennedy, a Democrat from Massachusetts, and Pete Domenici, a Republican from New Mexico, have proposed legislation to devote $75 million for suicide prevention, their bill never mentions guns, instead focusing on mental health.

Last February [1999], a subcommittee of the Senate Appropriations Committee held the first congressional hearing on suicide prevention. Surgeon General David Satcher was a witness at the hearing; [in 1999], Satcher declared suicide a serious public health threat and made it a top priority—becoming the first surgeon general ever to do so.

Gun control advocacy groups and suicide prevention organizations have been as uncoordinated as the NRA has been powerful.

At the Senate's February suicide hearings, however, guns were barely mentioned. And indeed, the Surgeon General's groundbreaking suicide report has been taken to task by the Bell Campaign, a gun violence prevention group, for virtually ignoring gun suicide. "How does a major national health report overlook the cause of 17,700 deaths?" asks a release put out by the organization. The release adds, "Surely Surgeon General David Satcher understands the need to address guns as part of any meaningful plan to prevent suicide. But, like his predecessors, the Surgeon General must go to Congress for research funding. And, as we all know, Cogress answers to the National Rifle Association."

The Campaign is right to implicate the NRA. Responding to those who charge that gun availability increases the chance of suicide, the NRA's Paul Blackman told *The Los Angeles Times*, "if a person is determined to kill himself, he will find a way." Not so, say some. As Emory University public health researcher Arthur Kellerman has written, "gun industry claims about the value of handguns for home defense are reminiscent of the early days of tobacco advertising, when cigarette companies extolled the health benefits of smoking."

In fact, the NRA is so determined to promote its viewpoint that it has found a way to quiet those who would publicize the facts that contradict it. (The organization did not return calls for this article.) The NRA successfully pressured Congress to cut funding for the Centers for Disease

Control's effort to understand the public health effects of guns.

Gun control advocacy groups and suicide prevention organizations have been as uncoordinated as the NRA has been powerful. Some suicide prevention groups don't even take gun control positions, like the Colorado-based Yellow Ribbon Foundation. Though the American Foundation for Suicide Prevention and the American Association of Suicidology take strong stances, the latter's executive director, Dr. Alan Berman, nevertheless calls suicide "the invisible kid sister" in the gun debate.

Few solutions

The result of this invisibility is that few have studied what kind of measures would specifically help reduce gun suicide. But some point to popular gun control proposals that could impact suicide levels—at least indirectly. Since many children and teenagers commit suicide with their parents' guns, experts say child trigger locks and smart gun technology (which would only allow a gun's owner to shoot it) would probably help prevent youth suicides. Likewise with President [Bill] Clinton's proposed safe storage law holding parents responsible for making loaded, unlocked guns available to children. On the other hand, the elderly are a high-risk group for suicide—and a group for whom many such measures would be less effective.

A few suggest a more controversial approach: expanding background checks for gun purchases to include mental health records. After all, more than 90 percent of suicides are connected to some type of mental or substance abuse disorder.

At present, federal law prohibits those who have been involuntarily committed to mental institutions from buying handguns. But law enforcement agencies do not have access to mental health records in most states, which means background checks frequently fail to prevent the mentally ill from buying guns. And that doesn't even begin to address those who have voluntarily entered mental institutions, or are simply receiving outpatient treatment. For these cases, many consider it crucial that at the very least, mental health professionals discuss the dangers of firearms with patients and their families.

Any discussion of using mental health records to prohibit people from buying guns raises a strong conflict, however. On the one hand, those concerned with suicide want to keep guns out of the hands of anyone who might consider it. On the other hand, some perceive such restrictions as unfair—and worry that expanding access to mental health records could violate patients' privacy.

The lack of proposals specifically designed to cut down on gun suicide only highlights the dearth of attention that the political and activist community has given the issue. Activists have treated suicide as a mental health issue only—excluding discussions of gun control to reduce suicide. And the NRA has ensured that the gun debate is centered on the criminal justice issue only—excluding discussions of gun control to reduce suicide.

But facts show that the debate must change. If stories like B.J. Stupak's begin to turn the debate toward the epidemic of gun suicide, perhaps the NRA will have to admit that a gun in the home is rarely a source of protection—and often leads to tragedy.

9

Stricter Gun Control Would Not Reduce Teen Suicide

Joseph P. Tartaro

Joseph P. Tartaro is executive editor of Gun Week.

Antigun activists distort statistics about teen gun deaths to support their agenda, and the media help to promote these distortions as facts. Advocacy groups such as Common Sense About Kids and Guns claim to be nonpolitical but are actually funded by antigun foundations. The increase in the number of children killed by gun accidents or gun suicides is in the single digits, so the advocacy groups use percentages to make the increase appear more dramatic. Antigun activists use distorted statistics in an attempt to remove guns from homes and prevent those who do not have guns from getting them.

Whenever the anti-gunners cook up a stew of numbers to support further restrictions on the lawful ownership of firearms, the media is always ready to serve that dish to an unsuspecting public.

Sometimes percentages are used when the real numbers don't count.

Sometimes the generic term "guns" is used when the numbers won't support an initiative against handguns.

These anti-gun stews have little basis in reality when it comes to public policy issues. They are intentionally concocted to support a pre-conceived agenda. And they are published in journals that cover the credentials of the so-called think tanks and policy analysts who confected them.

One of the latest of these was gobbled up by the news media and regurgitated under the headline, "Study Finds Gun Accidents, Suicides on Increase Among Children."

Contradictory facts

The headline seems to run contra to government and National Safety Council reports about homicides, suicides and accidents involving firearms which have been published in recent years. The numbers have been going down steadily, with the smallest reduction in suicides. In fact, the latest government figures indicate that there are substantially more suicides than homicides involving firearms. And the National Safety Council shows that the number of fatal firearms accidents—for children as well as the overall population—has dropped to the lowest level since such records were first published beginning near the start of the 1900s.

"Though overall firearm deaths are down nationwide, an analysis of gun accidents and suicides among kids finds that within certain age groups there were startling increases," the report on the study began.

"The greatest increases were among 5- to 9-year-olds, where the number of accidental firearm deaths increased 21% and among 10–14-year-olds, where there was a 21% increase in the number of firearm suicides.

"These findings were reported by Victoria Reggie Kennedy, president of the non-political gun safety and gun violence prevention organization Common Sense About Kids and Guns, on the one-year anniversary of the group's founding," the story continued. (Mrs. Kennedy is the wife of Sen. Edward Kennedy (D-MA).)

These anti-gun stews have little basis in reality when it comes to public policy issues.

The "Common Sense" group is one of many such advocacy groups funded by grants from anti-gun foundations that hope to direct public policy by claiming to be "non-political" while masking their real agenda. Another such group was formed in Boulder, CO, in October [2000].

"Common Sense highlighted national mortality statistics from the Center for Disease Control's (CDC) National Center for Health Statistics that showed how overall firearm deaths for children and teens (0–19) were down 10% in 1998, but non-homicide firearm deaths (i.e. accidents and suicides) only declined 4% from 1997 to 1998 (from 1,643 to 1,577)," the report continued.

"Common Sense, which focuses on parental responsibility for preventing kids' unsupervised access to guns, pointed out that in non-homicide categories, especially among younger kids, there were actually increases."

Real numbers

But when you look past the percentages at the real numbers, a different picture emerges.

The media reports said: "The study found that:
- "—For kids under 15, non-homicide firearm deaths increased 4% (from 283 to 295).
- "—Among 5–9-year-olds, accidental firearm deaths increased 21% (28 to 34).
- "—Among 10–14-year-olds, firearm suicides increased 21% (126 to 153)."

When you go back and look at the real numbers, you see that for kids under 15, non-homicide firearms deaths in the period increased by a total of 8 nationwide.

And among children between 5 and 9 years old, there was an actual increase of 6 in the total of accidental firearms deaths.

Long ago in journalism school, we were instructed to never say "only" in connection with any number of deaths. But in this case, "only" is relevant because it provides a more realistic evaluation of what "Common Sense" really has to say. Using such numbers to produce scary percentages is statistical tomfoolery. When the numbers themselves don't add up, and there is no significant trend, resort to percentages.

This is essentially the kind of reality that John Lott, senior researcher at Yale University, used to debunk the firearms accident claims of Gov. Parris Glendening in Maryland. The governor was promoting his trigger lock and "smart gun" legislation with inflated claims.

When Lott checked the numbers, he found that there had been two such incidents in the period the governor cited.

The job of the anti-gun think tanks is to come up with headlines that will change public opinion. If they have to fudge the numbers, they will do so.

The report on the "Common Sense" study eventually made it clear that the organization was promoting "safe firearms storage"—that is gun locks and "smart guns." But if they hadn't played with the numbers, they wouldn't have been able to promote their agenda at all. They needed a hook for their PR and percentages gave them one. How many headlines would they have gotten if they had started by saying that 8 or 6 more children in those age groups had been killed accidentally during their study period?

The job of the anti-gun think tanks is to come up with headlines that will change public opinion. If they have to fudge the numbers, they will do so.

While the first story was making headlines, another by Reuters "Health" news service, claimed that guns remain in homes of depressed teens. This so-called study is linked to the relatively new policy of some health professionals to intervene in the family affairs of patients with guns.

"Even after being told by a health professional that keeping a gun at home may increase the likelihood that a depressed child will attempt suicide, most parents of depressed teens do not remove firearms from their homes, according to a new study, Reuters said.

"The high proportion of families who, after receiving information, continued to keep a gun in the house is concerning, given the apparent risk for suicide conveyed by a gun in the home and the 30-fold increased risk for suicide conveyed by adolescent depression," Dr. David A. Brent and colleagues at the University of Pittsburgh in Pennsylvania wrote in the October issue of *The Journal of the American Academy of Child and Adolescent Psychiatry*.

"Based on research indicating that depressed teens who live in homes where a gun is present are more likely to attempt suicide than those living in firearm-free homes, Brent and his colleagues began asking parents of teens treated for depression in an outpatient clinic whether they had a gun at home. If the family did have a gun at home, parents were counseled on the suicide risks of keeping a gun at home and advised to remove the gun from the house. If there was not a gun in the home, however, the parents and patients were not counseled on the dangers of keeping a gun at home."

Gun-free zones

"Most parents did not heed the advice about making their homes gun-free zones, the researchers report. During a child's treatment and up to 2 years later, guns were removed from only one-fourth to one-third of the houses that had firearms.

"And some homes that were previously gun-free had firearms present at the end of the study. In fact, about one out of every six such households obtained a gun by the end of the 2-year follow-up period," the report claimed.

At this point, you might have guessed what the recommendation for future action would be, but here is what Reuters reported was the conclusion:

"The results of the study show that doctors and other health professionals need to do more to make parents of depressed teens aware of the risks of having a gun at home, including discussing the issue with families who do not have firearms to ensure that their homes remain gun-free, according to the researchers."

There you have it. These researchers don't want to merely remove guns, they also want to be sure the families that don't already have firearms don't become gunowners.

10

Antidepressants Can Prevent Teen Suicide

Suzanne Vogel-Scibilia

Suzanne Vogel-Scibilia is a psychiatrist and a member of the board of directors of the National Alliance for the Mentally Ill.

Access to selective serotonin reuptake inhibitors (SSRIs), a kind of antidepressant, for young people must be guaranteed. Research indicates that SSRIs can be effective in treating depression in young people, and there is no evidence that this medication increases the risk of suicide. Children with mental illnesses such as depression or bipolar disorder can benefit from comprehensive treatment plans that include SSRI medications.

Editor's Note: The following viewpoint was originally given as testimony before the Food and Drug Administration on February 2, 2004.

Good Morning. NAMI (the National Alliance for the Mentally Ill) greatly appreciates this opportunity to provide a statement on the critically important issue of the use of selective serotonin reuptake inhibitors (SSRIs) for children and adolescents with depression—specifically focused on reports of suicidality (ideation and attempts) in clinical trials and approaches to analyzing data from these trials and further research needs to address these issues.

NAMI was founded as a grassroots family advocacy movement 25 years ago in Madison, Wisconsin. Today, NAMI has more than 220,000 consumer and family members nationwide dedicated to improving the lives of children and adults living with mental illnesses.

My name is Suzanne Vogel-Scibilia and I am a member of the NAMI Board of Directors. As a person diagnosed with bipolar disorder, I am proud to serve on the NAMI Board and proud that NAMI is the nation's "voice on mental illness" representing both consumers and family members. I am also proud to be the mother of five children, two of who are diagnosed with mental illnesses and one of who is currently being treated with an SSRI.

Suzanne Vogel-Scibilia, testimony before the Food and Drug Administration Psychopharmacologic Drugs Advisory Committee and the Pediatric Subcommittee of the Anti-Infective Drugs Advisory Committee, Washington, DC, February 2, 2004.

I am also a psychiatrist with board certification in general psychiatry, addiction psychiatry and geriatric psychiatry and have additional board certification from the American Board of Adolescent Psychiatry. I have a thriving practice in Beaver, Pennsylvania.

My son, Anthony, has had severe mental illness, primarily depression and attention deficit disorder, as a manifestation of his bipolar disorder and another son has had treatment with numerous antidepressant medications including several SSRIs. My children have had tremendous improvement with their illnesses and lead very full and functional lives because of SSRI medication, along with other psychotropic medications. I shudder to think of their plight if these medications were not available.

I, as a mother and a psychiatrist, realize that the evidence linking suicidal behavior to [selective serotonin reuptake inhibitors] is weak and I will not draw conclusions lightly based on anecdotal information and isolated case reports.

One of my sons has had suicide attempts and violent incidents with knives. He has also run out of our house—in a fit of terror—in subzero weather only to be found freezing and hypothermic by our local police department in the next township. These incidents all occurred when his illness was not adequately treated with antidepressant medication. My other son suffers from disabling obsessive-compulsive disorder symptoms and depression and has had his life improve dramatically from treatment with SSRIs.

Many of my patients, as well as my children, have had severe symptoms from their illness that others may claim is from the treatment. I, as a mother and a psychiatrist, realize that the evidence linking suicidal behavior to SSRIs is weak and I will not draw conclusions lightly based on anecdotal information and isolated case reports. As a psychiatrist, I question whether some of the cases where a child worsened on SSRIs may have been because the child had bipolar disorder instead of unipolar depression. This has been posited by authorities in the field as well (American College of Neuropsychopharmacology Report to the FDA, dated January 21, 2004).

Upon review of the research, which confirms the experience of many NAMI families, NAMI believes that SSRI access for young people should be maintained.

Increased research on early onset mental illnesses

The prevalence of mental illnesses in children and adolescents is significant and on the rise. Research shows that early identification and comprehensive treatment can improve the long-term prognosis of children with mental illnesses. Research on the effectiveness of treatments—including SSRIs and other psychotropic medications—is our best hope for the future.

With so many children and adolescents being prescribed psychotropic medications, we need research and science to help guide the safe and effective use of these medications. There is an essential need for more data on the long-term effects and safety of psychotropic medication use in children. NAMI calls on NIMH [National Institute of Mental Health] to make a significant investment in research on early onset mental disorders and the use of psychotropic medications—including SSRIs—for children and adolescents. This promises to help us understand the safety and effectiveness of SSRIs and other psychotropic medications in treating mental illnesses in children.

The discussion about children and adolescents and the use of SSRIs to treat depression must also address the critical need to ensure that all children and adolescents with mental illnesses have access to evidence-based assessments and interventions—with quality clinical care as an integral part of all aspects of the service delivery system. An expanded reporting system is necessary so that data from the pharmaceutical industry and other studies is available to the public.

For children with mental illnesses—especially those with persistent and serious mental illnesses—the ability to access psychiatric medications when needed is vital. NAMI believes that many children with mental illnesses need access to medication as part of a comprehensive treatment plan. NAMI is concerned that any limitations on the ability of knowledgeable practitioners to treat children with SSRIs, when needed, could be damaging to children in our country especially those with serious life altering illnesses.

The efficacy of psychotropic medications for children

Parents' or caregivers' decisions about whether to use SSRIs or other psychotropic medications for their child can be extremely difficult. Psychotropic medications for young children with mental illnesses should be used only when the anticipated benefits outweigh the risks. Parents and family members should be fully informed of the risks and expected benefits associated with medications prescribed for children and decisions about whether to use medication for a child should only be made after carefully weighing these factors. Children and adolescents who are taking psychotropic medications must be closely monitored and frequently evaluated by qualified mental health providers.

With so many children and adolescents being prescribed psychotropic medications, we need research and science to help guide the safe and effective use of these medications.

At the same time, psychotropic medications, including SSRIs, have been lifesaving for many children with mental illnesses. Families often report that the use of medication, either alone or along with other treatment modalities, has allowed their child to participate in school like other children, to live at home and to develop friendships with peers. We also know that the lack of effective treatment for a child or adolescent who needs it will adversely affect the child's overall physical and mental development, including the ability to learn, develop self-esteem, socialize and function in the community.

I have seen, along with many other clinicians, children respond positively to SSRIs—some dramatically. Moreover, there is little research on the outcomes that result from an absence of treatment, although lack of treatment undoubtedly leads to a greater number of preventable tragedies. SSRIs have actually been found to be effective in several recent reports while a large meta-analysis of an older alternative antidepressant family, the tricyclic antidepressants, failed to show the same improvements.

Let us not forget that medications have been shown to be effective and no studies have proven that [selective serotonin reuptake inhibitors] cause suicide or suicidal behavior in young people.

Another possible treatment alternative to SSRIs is cognitive-behavioral therapy (CBT), a form of psychotherapy. However, CBT has had a high treatment non-response rate for some children with depression, which provides yet another reason to have alternative treatments, like medications, available for children.

Many long-term studies show that the treatment of childhood onset depression with psychotherapy, medication or both improves the social and educational outcomes and emotional health of our children.

Suicide and the consequences of untreated mental illnesses

We are pleased that the FDA [Food and Drug Administration] is looking closely at the data related to SSRI use and suicidality. NAMI is deeply concerned with the public health crisis in the number of youth who commit suicide. We are also alarmed by the high number of youth with mental illnesses that fail to receive any treatment or services. The U.S. Surgeon General reports that up to 80% of youth who need mental health treatment fail to receive any treatment.

NAMI families are well aware of the tragic consequences of untreated mental illnesses in youth. Suicide is the third leading cause of death in adolescents aged 15 to 24. Evidence strongly suggests that as many as 90% of those who commit suicide have a diagnosable mental disorder.

Youth with untreated mental illnesses also tragically end up in jails and prisons—research shows that 65% of boys and 75% of girls in juvenile detention have at least one psychiatric diagnosis. They fail or drop out of school—leading to a greatly diminished future as citizens and productive workers.

Educators have found that children with a mental health disability—including depression—are most likely to flounder in the educational system and have lifelong complications from the lack of education if not adequately treated for their depressive symptoms. The risk of conduct problems and addictive behavior increases dramatically if any person with mental illness is not adequately treated.

The shortage of child and
adolescent mental health providers

Families across the country also struggle with accessing mental health treatment for their child because of the crisis in the shortage of child and adolescent mental health providers—especially child-trained psychiatrists. The importance of a strong relationship between families and clinicians cannot be overstated; it is especially imperative in cases involving children and adolescents with depression.

The tragic reality is that the shortage of child and adolescent psychiatrists in this country—especially in rural communities—makes it extremely difficult for families to access appropriate and effective treatment for their child with a mental illness. These issues must be considered in the context of this discussion on the safety and efficacy of SSRIs to treat children and adolescents with depression.

In summary, I would like to thank the committee for allowing NAMI to share our views on these critically important issues. The families that we represent from across the country call for increased research and data to understand the long- and short-term safety and efficacy of SSRIs to treat children and adolescents with depression. Let us not forget that medications have been shown to be effective and no studies have proven that SSRIs cause suicide or suicidal behavior in young people. In fact, data suggest that SSRI use may have decreased suicides among young people, which is a critical public health problem.

NAMI is aware that not all of the data concerning the impact of SSRIs in children and adolescents has been made available to the public and independent researchers. It is critical that all such data be made available so that families everywhere can make decisions about treatment based on full knowledge of the risks and benefits. But we cannot stop there. Even if families and clinicians could make fully informed decisions about the use of SSRIs in a child, many families do not have access to providers. Services are woefully inadequate around the nation. And the current state of knowledge is simply inadequate—we need to understand mental illnesses in children much better and we need better treatments. If the FDA and U.S. federal government truly care about the well-being of American children with mental illnesses, it would address all of these issues.

11

Antidepressants Can Lead to Teen Suicide

Part I: Robert Fritz; Part II: Tom Woodward; Part III: Vera Sharav

Robert Fritz and Tom Woodward are parents of children who committed suicide while on selective serotonin reuptake inhibitors. Vera Sharav is president of the Alliance for Human Research Protection.

The Food and Drug Administration (FDA) has been aware that selective serotonin reuptake inhibitors (SSRIs), a type of antidepressant, increase the risk of suicide in children, but it has failed to warn the public. This has led to the tragic deaths of many teenagers. The interests of the drug companies are being put ahead of the public's, and it is time that the FDA take action to prevent additional unnecessary deaths.

Editor's Note: This three-part viewpoint consists of statements by three witnesses testifying before the Food and Drug Administration Psychopharmacologic Drugs Advisory Committee and the Pediatric Subcommittee of the Anti-Infective Drugs Advisory Committee on February 2, 2004. Due to the large number of public witnesses, statements were limited to two minutes each.

Part I

People have been pleading with the FDA [Food and Drug Administration] for 11-plus years to put warnings on prescriptions for antidepression medication to no avail. The FDA has had people present information about suicidal tendency increase and numerous completed suicides, and still no warnings of increased risk of suicide were issued. The people of the United States have a right to know what risks are associated with taking these drugs. I have a right to know what risks are associated with taking these drugs, so I can make an informed decision as to whether or not I want my children to take these drugs. The need for a warning is compounded by the fact that doctors are prescribing these medications off la-

Robert Fritz, Tom Woodward, and Vera Sharav, testimony before the Food and Drug Administration Psychopharmacologic Drugs Advisory Committee and the Pediatric Subcommittee of the Anti-Infective Drugs Advisory Committee, Washington, DC, February 2, 2004.

bel. My daughter, Stephanie Raye Fritz, was taking Zoloft [a type of selective serotonin reuptake inhibitor (SSRI)]. We weren't told of any risk of increased suicidal tendencies or increased suicide attempts. She hung herself . . . in her bedroom after finishing her homework. She showed no signs of increased depression or imminent suicidal thoughts, and, in fact, was still recruiting people to see her sing the following month. We had no warning of what Zoloft could do to our daughter, but you people, the FDA, certainly did. . . . Two weeks before she took her life, you put out a Public Health Advisory and notified physicians about preliminary data from studies suggesting an excess of reported suicidal ideation and suicide attempts for pediatric patients receiving certain of these antidepressant drugs. Why weren't we, the parents of the kids taking Zoloft, notified with this advisory? It is too late for my daughter, but for the FDA to continue to sit on this information and not let the public know the risks associated with these drugs is a gross misuse of power. I am not asking that these drugs be taken off the market. I don't know enough about their safety to recommend that. What I am seeking is that when the drugs are prescribed off label, or when drugs are prescribed after an advisory is issued suggesting new adverse side effects, that the FDA make it mandatory that the physicians prescribing such drugs explain in plain English what the risks are and that an informed written consent be received from the parents or the patient's guardian. I hope that you will agree that all Americans deserve to know what risks they are assuming when they take medication. I believe that most Americans, including most elected officials, agree with that. How many more people have to die before a warning gets issued?

Part II

My name is Tom Woodward. My wife Kathy and I have been married for 19 years and until 6 months ago had 4 children. Our oldest child, Julie, hung herself after 7 days on Zoloft, and she was only 17, was a cautious child, and had no history of self-harm or suicide, nor was there any history of depression or suicide in our family. The doctors we spoke with stressed that Zoloft was safe and had very few side effects. The possibility of violence, self-harm, or suicidal acts was never raised. The two and a half pages we received with the Zoloft never mentioned self-harm or suicide. Julie began experiencing akathisia [extreme agitation and restlessness] almost immediately. We now know from a blood test from the coroner's office that she was not metabolizing the drug. We are 100 percent convinced that Zoloft killed our daughter. We are here because we believe the system we have in place is flawed. It is clear that the FDA is a political entity and its leadership has protected the economic interests of the drug industry. Under the Bush administration, the FDA has placed the interests of the drug industry over protecting the American public. . . . Eighty-six percent of the $14 million in political contributions given by drug companies has gone to the Bush administration Republican candidates—what did Pfizer, Eli Lilly, and GlaxoSmithKline Beecham buy? The FDA should be a jealous advocate in protecting the American people. Those in leadership positions within the FDA must be beyond reproach. FDA's chief counsel Daniel Troy has spent his career defending the drug industry. Suppressing unfavorable data may be legal, but is it ethical? If the trials don't favor a drug, the public never hears of them. Legal maneuverings have thrown out the scientific method. The drug industry must be compelled to produce all of their findings and studies. I also believe public funding of these trials is warranted. Our daughter, Julie, had been excited about college and scored 1,300 in her SATs several weeks before her death. Instead of picking out colleges with our daughter, my wife and I had to pick out a cemetery plot for her. Instead of looking forward to visiting Julie at school, we now visit her grave. The loss we have experienced is horrific. We don't want another innocent child or family to suffer this tragedy.

Part III

I am Vera Sharav and I am a resident of the Alliance for Human Research Protection. The family testimonies that you are hearing today are not anecdotes. They are corroborated by a Harvard review of children's medical charts, which found that within three months of treatment on an SSRI, 22 percent suffered drug-induced adverse psychiatric effects, and overall, 74 percent of children suffered adverse events during the course of treatment. The FDA has known for years, but failed to reveal that antidepressants consistently fail to demonstrate a benefit in children. At least 12 of 15 trials failed. The FDA has known and failed to warn physicians and the public that SSRIs increase the risk of suicide and hostility in children. FDA's 1996 Zoloft review found "7-fold greater incidence of suicidality in children treated with Zoloft than adults." The British Drug Regulatory Authority reviewed the evidence, which is not being shown in this meeting, and they determined that the risks far outweigh any benefits. They took action to protect children. When is the FDA going to take action? The FDA is foot dragging, equivocating, and tinkering with definitions while children are dying. The *San Francisco Chronicle* reports that the FDA has barred its own medical reviewer who reviewed more than 20 trials involving 4,000 children, and his findings confirmed the British finding, which is that SSRIs increase the risk of suicide.

12

Pediatricians Should Try to Identify Suicidal Teens

American Academy of Pediatrics
Committee on Adolescence

The American Academy of Pediatrics (AAP), Committee on Adolescence and its member pediatricians dedicate their efforts and resources to the health, safety, and well-being of infants, children, adolescents, and young adults.

Pediatricians can help prevent adolescent suicide by knowing the symptoms of depression and other presuicidal behavior. The extent to which pediatricians can provide appropriate care for suicidal adolescents depends on their knowledge, skill, comfort with the topic, and ready access to appropriate community resources. All teenagers with suicidal symptoms should know that their pleas for assistance are heard and that pediatricians are willing to serve as advocates to help them resolve their problems.

The number of adolescent deaths from suicide in the United States has increased dramatically during the past few decades. In 1997, there were 4186 suicides among people 15 to 24 years old, 1802 suicides among those 15 to 19 years old, and 2384 among those 20 to 24 years old. In 1997, 13% of all deaths in the 15- through 24-year-old age group were attributable to suicide. The true number of deaths from suicide actually may be higher, because some of these deaths are recorded as "accidental."

From 1950 to 1990, the suicide rate for adolescents in the 15- to 19-year-old group increased by 300%. Adolescent males 15 to 19 years old had a rate 6 times greater than the rate for females. The ratio of attempted suicides to completed suicides among adolescents is estimated to be 50:1 to 100:1, and the incidence of unsuccessful suicide attempts is higher among females than among males. Suicide affects young people from all races and socioeconomic groups, although some groups seem to have higher rates than others. Native American males have the highest suicide rate, African American women the lowest. A statewide survey of students in grades 7 through 12 found that 28.1% of bisexual and homosexual males and 20.5% of bisexual and homosexual females had reported at-

American Academy of Pediatrics, Committee on Adolescence, "Suicide and Suicide Attempts in Adolescents," *Pediatrics*, vol. 105, April 2000, pp. 871–74. Copyright © 2000 by the American Academy of Pediatrics. Reproduced with permission.

tempting suicide. The National Youth Risk Behavior Survey of students in grades 9 through 12 indicated that nearly one fourth (24.1%) of students had seriously considered attempting suicide during the 12 months preceding the survey, 17.7% had made a specific plan, and 8.7% had made an attempt.

Firearms, used in [more than] 67% of suicides, are the leading cause of death for males and females who commit suicide. More than 90% of suicide attempts involving a firearm are fatal because there is little chance for rescue. Firearms in the home, regardless of whether they are kept unloaded or stored locked up, are associated with a higher risk for adolescent suicide. Parents must be warned about the lethality of firearms in the home and be advised strongly to remove them from the premises. Ingestion of pills is the most common method among adolescents who attempt suicide.

From 1950 to 1990, the suicide rate for adolescents in the 15- to 19-year-old group increased by 300%.

Youth, who seem to be at much greater risk from media exposure than adults, may imitate suicidal behavior seen on television. Media coverage of a teenage suicide may lead to cluster suicides, additional deaths from suicides in youths within a 1- to 2-week period afterward.

Adolescents at increased risk

Although no specific tests are capable of identifying suicidal persons, specific risk factors exist. Adolescents at higher risk commonly have a history of depression, a previous suicide attempt, a family history of psychiatric disorders (especially depression and suicidal behavior), family disruption, and certain chronic or debilitating physical disorders or psychiatric illness. Alcohol use and alcoholism indicate high risk for suicide. Alcohol use has been associated with 50% of suicides. Living out of the home (in a correctional facility or group home) and a history of physical or sexual abuse are additional factors more commonly found in adolescents who exhibit suicidal behavior. Psychosocial problems and stresses, such as conflicts with parents, breakup of a relationship, school difficulties or failure, legal difficulties, social isolation, and physical ailments (including hypochondriacal preoccupation), commonly are reported or observed in young people who attempt suicide. These precipitating factors often are cited by youths as reasons for attempting suicide. Gay and bisexual adolescents have been reported to exhibit high rates of depression and have been reported to have rates of suicidal ideation and attempts 3 times higher than other adolescents. Studies of twins show that monozygotic twins show significantly higher concordance for suicide than dizygotic twins. Long-term high levels of community violence may contribute to emotional and conduct problems and add to the risk of suicide for exposed youth. Adolescent and parent questionnaires that cover those risk factors listed above, may be useful in the office setting to assist in obtaining a complete history.

Approaching the adolescent

All adolescents with symptoms of depression should be asked about suicidal ideation, and an estimation of the degree of suicidal intent should
be made. No data indicate that inquiry about suicide precipitates the behavior. In fact, adolescents often are relieved that someone has heard
their cry for help. For most adolescents, this cry for help represents an attempt to resolve a difficult conflict, escape an intolerable living situation,
make someone understand their desperate feelings, or make someone feel
sorry or guilty. Suicidal thoughts or comments should never be dismissed
as unimportant. Adolescents must be told by pediatricians that their plea
for assistance has been heard and that they will be helped.

Serious depression in adolescents may manifest in several ways. For
some adolescents, symptoms may be similar to those in adults, with signs,
such as depressed mood almost every day, crying spells or inability to cry,
discouragement, irritability, a sense of emptiness and meaninglessness,
negative expectations of self and the environment, low self-esteem, isolation, a feeling of helplessness, markedly diminished interest or pleasure in
most activities, significant weight loss or weight gain, insomnia or hyper-
somnia, fatigue or loss of energy, feelings of worthlessness, and diminished
ability to think or concentrate. However, it is more common for an adolescent with serious depression to exhibit psychosomatic symptoms or behavioral problems. Such a teenager may seek care for recurrent or persistent complaints, such as abdominal pain, chest pain, headache, lethargy,
weight loss, dizziness and syncope, or other nonspecific symptoms. Behavioral problems that may be manifestations of masked depression include truancy, deterioration in academic performance, running away from
home, defiance of authorities, self-destructive behavior, vandalism, alcohol and other drug abuse, sexual acting out, and delinquency. Episodic de-
spondency leading to self-destructive acts can occur in any adolescent, including high achievers. These adolescents may believe that they have
failed or disappointed their parents and family and perceive suicide as
their only option. Other adolescents may believe that suicide is a better option than life as they experience it.

---

*Parents must be warned about the lethality of
firearms in the home and be advised strongly to
remove them from the premises.*

One approach to initiate an inquiry into suicidal thoughts or concerns is to ask a general question, such as "Have you ever felt so unhappy
or depressed that you thought about killing yourself or wished you were
dead?" If the response is positive, the pediatrician should inquire about
thoughts of death, thoughts of suicide, suicide plans (eg, method, time,
and place), securing the available means (eg, guns and ropes), previous attempts (and whether the attempts were discovered), and the response of
the family. These basic questions can help pediatricians construct an assessment of suicidal risk. In addition, they should assess individual coping resources, accessible support systems, and attitudes of the adolescent

and family toward intervention and follow-up.

Although confidentiality is important in adolescent health care, for adolescents at risk to themselves or others, confidentiality must be breached. Pediatricians need to inform the appropriate persons when they believe an adolescent is at risk of suicide. In all cases, determination of the sequence of events that preceded the threat, identification of current problems and conflicts, and assessment of the degree of suicidal intent must be completed.

Management of the suicidal adolescent

Adolescents with a well-thought-out plan that includes method, place, time, and clear intent are at high risk. The degree of intent can be inferred from the actual and perceived lethality of the intended means. Use of firearms, for example, has a high degree of lethality and poor chance of rescue. An adolescent who takes pills in the presence of others, however, has a good chance of rescue. Even adolescents who initially may seem at low risk, joke about suicide, or seek treatment for repeated somatic complaints may be asking for help the only way they can. Their concerns should be assessed thoroughly and follow-up arranged for additional evaluation and treatment. For adolescents who seem to be at moderate or high risk for suicide or have attempted suicide, a mental health professional should be consulted immediately during the office visit. Options for immediate evaluation include hospitalization, transfer to an emergency department, or an appointment the same day with a mental health professional.

All adolescents with symptoms of depression should be asked about suicidal ideation, and an estimation of the degree of suicidal intent should be made.

The safest course of action is hospitalization, placing the adolescent in a safe and protected environment. An inpatient stay will allow time for a complete medical and psychiatric or psychologic evaluation and initiation of therapy in a controlled setting. The choice of hospital unit depends on available facilities in the area, health and mental health insurance, and managed care policies. Adolescent medicine units must be staffed to manage the medical and psychiatric needs of suicidal adolescents. Proper medical intervention and treatment are essential for stabilization and management of patients' conditions. After the adolescent's condition has been stabilized medically, a comprehensive emotional and psychosocial assessment must be initiated before discharge. Inquiry should be made into the events that preceded the attempt, the adolescent's current problems, and the presence of current or previous psychiatric illness and self-destructive behavior. In addition to an in-depth psychological evaluation of the adolescent, family members should be interviewed to obtain additional information to help explain the adolescent's suicidal thoughts or attempt. This information includes detailed questions about the adolescent's medical, emotional, social, and family history with special attention to signs and symptoms of depression, stress, and substance abuse. With parental permission and adolescent assent, teachers and family friends also may provide useful information if confidentiality is not breached.

Intervention should be tailored to the adolescent's needs. Adolescents with a responsive intact family, good peer relations and social support, hope for the future, and a desire to resolve conflicts may require only brief crisis-oriented intervention. In contrast, adolescents who have made previous attempts, exhibit a high degree of intent to commit suicide, show evidence of serious depression or other psychiatric illness, are abusing alcohol and other drugs, and have families who are unwilling to commit to counseling are at high risk and may require psychiatric hospitalization.

The safest course of action is hospitalization, placing the adolescent in a safe and protected environment.

All adolescents who attempt suicide need a comprehensive outpatient treatment plan before discharge. Specific plans are needed because compliance with outpatient therapy often is poor. Most adolescents examined in emergency rooms and referred to outpatient facilities fail to keep their appointments. This is especially true when the appointment is made with someone other than the family pediatrician or the person who performed the initial assessment. Continuity of care is, therefore, of paramount importance. Pediatricians can enhance continuity and compliance by maintaining contact with suicidal adolescents even after referrals are made. All firearms should be removed from the home because adolescents may still find access to locked guns stored in the home.

Adolescents judged not to be at high risk for suicide should be followed up closely, referred for mental health evaluation in a timely manner, or both.

Recommendations

1. Pediatricians need to know the risk factors (eg, signs and symptoms of depression) associated with adolescent suicide and serve as a resource for parents, teachers, school personnel, clergy, and community groups that work with youth about the issue of adolescent suicide.
2. Pediatricians should ask questions about depression, suicidal thoughts, and other risk factors associated with suicide in routine history-taking throughout adolescence.
3. During routine evaluations, pediatricians need to ask whether firearms are kept in the home and discuss with parents the risks of firearms as specifically related to adolescent suicide. Specifically for adolescents at risk of suicide, parents should be advised to remove guns and ammunition from the house.
4. Pediatricians should recognize the medical and psychiatric needs of the suicidal adolescent and work closely with families and health

care professionals involved in the management and follow-up of youth who are at risk or have attempted suicide.

5. Pediatricians should become familiar with community, state, and national resources that are concerned with youth suicide, including mental health agencies, family and children's services, crisis hotlines, and crisis intervention centers. Working relationships should be developed with colleagues in child and adolescent psychiatry, clinical psychology, and other mental health professions to manage the care of adolescents at risk for suicide optimally. Because mental and physical health services are often provided through different systems of care, extra effort is necessary to assure good communication, continuity, and follow-up.

6. Pediatricians should advocate for benefit packages in health insurance plans to assure that adolescents have access to preventive and therapeutic mental health services that adequately cover the treatment of clinically significant mental health disorders.

13

A Three-Stage Screening Strategy Can Prevent Teen Suicide

David Shaffer

David Shaffer is the Irving Philips Professor of Psychiatry and the director of child and adolescent psychiatry in the Department of Psychiatry at Columbia University's College of Physicians and Surgeons. He trained in medicine and psychiatry at the University of London and is a fellow of both the Royal College of Psychiatrists and the Royal College of Physicians.

Adolescent suicide is a serious public health problem. Ninety percent of suicide victims have a diagnosable psychiatric disorder at the time of their death; therefore, the most effective method of preventing teen suicides is to find at-risk individuals and provide them with treatment. Many screening strategies have been tried in school settings, but only the three-stage method has proved effective in identifying at-risk teens and directing them to help. During the first stage, students complete a self-report questionnaire; if their answers indicate elevated risk, they move on to the second phase of the process, during which they participate in a computerized diagnostic interview. Finally, if this test shows high susceptibility to suicide, the student is sent to a clinician who makes a face-to-face evaluation and arranges intervention if needed.

A dolescent suicide is an important public health problem. Each year in the United States, between 2000 and 2500 adolescents under the age of 20 commit suicide. Almost twice as many adolescents commit suicide than die from all natural causes combined. Adolescent suicide prevention is therefore an important goal, which is most likely to be achieved by a better understanding of risk factors and how and when they operate. This article summarizes relevant aspects of what is known about the origins and development of suicidality and suggests ways in which the problem could be reduced.

David Shaffer, "Methods of Adolescent Suicide Prevention," *Journal of Clinical Psychiatry*, vol. 60, 1999, pp. 70–74. Copyright © 1999 by the *Journal of Clinical Psychiatry*. Reproduced by permission.

Risk factors

Much of what we know about the characteristics of adolescents who commit suicide is derived from epidemiologically based psychological-autopsy studies. In a study of that kind that we conducted, we examined 120 of 170 consecutive suicides completed by individuals 20 years of age and younger within a 2-year period in New York, New Jersey, and Connecticut, along with 147 control subjects matched for age, ethnicity, and sex. We found that 90% of suicide victims had a diagnosable psychiatric disorder at the time of their death, and more than half of these individuals had experienced significant symptoms for longer than 2 years. . . . The principal psychiatric risk factors were a past suicide attempt (approximately one third of suicide victims had made a previous suicide attempt); symptoms of a mood disorder (approximately 40% of the victims suffered from an affective disorder); and substance abuse, which was frequently comorbid with a mood disorder (approximately one quarter of all suicide victims and two thirds of older males abused substances). Conduct disorder was also common in suicide victims, but was present in many controls, and thus did not emerge as a significant risk factor. About half of the suicide victims had been in contact with a mental health professional prior to committing suicide. In most cases, however, the psychiatric attendance was for a suicide attempt and not for the treatment of mood symptoms.

We found that 90% of suicide victims had a diagnosable psychiatric disorder at the time of their death.

This study also examined risk factors in the family environment, such as conflict between parents and between parents and children, and other measures of family disruption. After controlling for psychiatric disorder in parents and children, differences on most of these measures were quite trivial, except for a low level of parent-child communication in the suicide victims. No significant differences were found in socioeconomic status between the suicide and control groups. Overall, the findings of this work suggest that a mood disorder and/or a prior suicide attempt are far more important risk factors for suicide than family factors.

Another strand of research focuses on the neurobiology of suicide. Systematic autopsy and in vivo studies have consistently found an elevated risk for suicide to be associated with abnormally low levels of the serotonin metabolites 5-hydroxyindoleacetic acid (5-HIAA) and homovanillic acid (HVA), a reduced concentration of 5-HT transporter enzymes in the prefrontal cortex, reduced presynaptic 5-HT receptor density, and increased postsynaptic 5-HT receptor density. These elements are thought to be associated with impulsive and volatile mood behaviors. It should be noted, however, that these findings have been demonstrated only in teenagers aged 16 and over, and it is not known what proportion of attempters have these abnormalities, nor whether these trait characteristics are stable or change as a function of psychiatric state.

Neuropsychiatric disorders are not the only factors that create risk for suicide. It appears that knowing about one suicide may facilitate suicidal behavior in others as a function of contagion or imitation. There is evidence that this process may take several different forms, including suicide epidemics or clusters, or as an aftereffect of news or fictional coverage of suicide.

In a study conducted by [Madelyn Gould, PhD and David Shaffer], the number of attempted and completed suicides made by adolescents in the metropolitan New York area after the broadcasting of 3 of 4 fictional television movies about suicide significantly increased compared with a baseline measurement. A second study extended the same investigation to 3 additional cities. Although the results of this examination did not fully replicate those evidenced in the first study, a significant effect was found in 1 of the 3 cities examined. This suggests that, while fictional accounts of suicide do, in fact, influence suicidal behavior, their effect interacts with other contextual factors.

A model for suicide prevention

Taken together, these findings lend themselves to an heuristic model for suicide prevention. This model proposes that, in order to commit suicide, an underlying condition, such as a mood disorder, substance abuse, and/or aggressive traits, must be present. The suicide act itself will usually be preceded by a stress event that will often have been a result of the underlying condition. Commonly, stress events in adolescence are disciplinary crises, being in trouble with the law or at school, or the loss of a relationship. Psychological autopsy studies suggest that the stress commonly leads to extreme anticipatory anxiety, and it seems as if suicide is in some cases an avoidant response to this effect.

The risk conditions and their immediate consequences are not uncommon, and, in most instances, the chain of events does not lead to suicide. Piecing together evidence from a variety of studies, we can postulate that inhibitory and facilitating factors come into play after the precipitating event and that the balance between them will determine whether the outcome is fatal or otherwise. Inhibiting factors that make suicide less likely include living in a culture in which suicide is strongly taboo, having available support or the presence of others, and having a sloweddown mental state. Conversely, the presence of other factors may facilitate suicide. These include living in a culture in which taboos about suicide are weak, having ready access to weapons or other methods of suicide, learning of a recent example of suicide by hearsay or in the media, being in an agitated or excited state, and being alone.

About half of the suicide victims had been in contact with a mental health professional prior to committing suicide.

This model suggests a number of prevention strategies. At the tail-end of the process, weapon control or media guidelines might reduce risk. While method control appears to be an obvious and realistic choice, research indicates such efforts produce negligible effects. A recent study examined the efficacy of this method by looking at the impact of gun-safe storage laws in 12 states on the gun-related deaths of children under the age of 15. While the rate of accidental shooting deaths decreased by 23% after the introduction of these laws, neither the gun-related homicide nor suicide rates showed statistically significant declines. There is not a great deal of research in this area, but what does exist indicates that method control might not be the most profitable approach to suicide prevention.

> *The suicide act itself will usually be preceded by a stress event that will often have been a result of the underlying condition.*

The Centers for Disease Control and Prevention (CDC) convened a national workshop to address the problem of communicability and generated preventative guidelines for media professionals to minimize suicide facilitation. To date, no studies have been done to demonstrate the efficacy of the CDC's guidelines. But, if successful, the frequent turnover of editorial staff would require continuous reeducation.

Hot lines and crisis services are designed to intervene at the penultimate stage before suicide, at a time when the suicidal person is most vulnerable. While these readily available services have the potential to positively affect mental state in the midst of a stress event or acute mood change, research suggests that they have little impact on suicide rates in the community. There may be several reasons for this. First, hot lines fail to reach those at greatest risk. Suicide is a predominantly male behavior, but most hot line callers and crisis-service users are female and not suicidal. Second, suicide is most often an impulsive act. As a result, many victims do not take the time to fully ponder other alternatives, such as reaching out for help from a trained crisis counselor. Third, it has been demonstrated that crisis services often give inappropriate advice. Research conducted on what is said and the circumstances that transpire when calls are placed to hot lines reveals a tendency toward the provision of generic advice regardless of the callers' problems. Crisis services and hot lines are readily available, however, and may have the potential to be enhanced by appropriate advertising and training in more varied responses.

At the most distant point on the flow diagram, suicide prevention would involve finding individuals who are at risk for suicide and providing them with treatment regardless of their current degree of suicidality.

Suicide prevention screening methods

Broadly speaking, there are 3 case-finding strategies that can be employed to this end. The first, commonly practiced in the United States, educates high school students about suicide in a way that is designed to reduce its stigma and to promote self-referral. The second is to educate those who encounter adolescents—teachers, parents, or other teens—and teach them how to identify individuals at risk and how to establish a connection with an appropriate source of help. The third strategy is direct screening, in which teenagers themselves are asked to indicate their mood and whether or not they are suicidal. Their replies are examined, and, if abnormal, the teenagers are referred for clinical care.

Two studies of note have examined the educational strategy of casefinding by destigmatization. The first study examined the impact of 3 school-based suicide-prevention programs administered to 758 high school students and 680 controls matched for age, ethnicity, and socioeconomic status. The results of this investigation revealed that, although most students found the suicide prevention programs to be helpful and informative, their implementation did not significantly increase knowledge, self-identification, or help-seeking behavior.

An 18-month follow-up study was conducted on these students in order to ascertain the long-term impact of the above-mentioned school-based suicide-prevention curricula. One hundred seventy-four of the high school students and 207 of the controls participated in the follow-up, which failed to provide adequate evidence of the programs' effects. In fact, students who were exposed to the programs were significantly less likely than controls to seek help for a serious personal or emotional problem. They were also significantly less likely to encourage a depressed or troubled friend to seek professional help. Another result of the study was that the students' model of suicide was negatively affected by the prevention program; that is, those students who entered the program believing that suicide was not a reasonable response to stress were more likely to change their minds after program delivery and consider suicide an understandable, possibly reasonable response to stress. The results of the original and follow-up studies suggest that destigmatization programs commonly practiced in educational settings are not effective.

Directly screening teenagers to identify those at high risk is not only efficient, but it is also cost effective.

The second educational strategy, that of educating third parties, such as teachers, parents, and peers, to identify those at risk for suicide and to then refer them for treatment, while logical in principle, is problematic in practice. Very often, there is an absence of external signs of suicidality or depression. Furthermore, the "warning" signs that are taught to parents, teachers, and peers, such as declining grades, social withdrawal, and loss of interest are highly nonspecific. If students are trained to look for potentially problematic and risky behavior in their peers and then offer advice, we are in effect promoting a highly intrusive and, most likely, very inaccurate intervention.

The three-stage screening process

The third approach, while it may take place in a school setting, is a strategy that does not have an educational component. This approach, a self-administered method of direct screening, differs from the 2 previous methods in that it does not involve suicide-awareness lectures or charge students and teachers with the task of acting like mental health professionals. Instead, it involves systematic screening for the predictors of suicide in general high school populations. Students are asked directly and confidentially whether they are experiencing any symptoms of depression, have suicidal ideation or have ever made a suicide attempt, and/or have an alcohol- or substance-abuse problem.

The most recent adolescent suicide statistics available may give cause for encouragement.

In our hands, this suicide-prevention method employs a 3-stage screening process. In the first stage, students complete a brief self-report questionnaire, the Columbia Teen Screen, in a health-related class. On the basis of their answers, students who might be at an elevated level of risk are advanced to the second phase of the process and further assessed through the employment of a computerized diagnostic interview, the DISC (Diagnostic Interview Schedule for Children), which can be administered by lay interviewers at relatively low cost. One of the many benefits of the 2-stage process generally, and that of the DISC specifically, is that it reduces the number of students who have to be seen by a clinician by screening out those students who are not at risk. At the end of each DISC interview, the computer generates a diagnostic report that is presented to a clinician who interviews students personally in the third and final stage of the screening process. The purpose of this face-to-face clinical interview is to determine whether or not the identified student needs to be referred for treatment or further evaluation. Those considered to be at high risk for suicide are students who admit to a suicide attempt or recent ideation, have either major depressive disorder or dysthymic disorder, or have an alcohol- or substance-abuse problem. Finally, a case manager contacts the students' parents in order to assist students who are deemed to be in need of additional intervention and also to ensure treatment compliance.

A 1996 study examined the efficacy of this suicide-prevention method in 2004 teenagers from New York metropolitan area high schools. Five hundred forty-six of the total number screened had a positive Columbia Teen Screen; that is, they met at least 1 of the positive-screening criteria for depression, dysthymia, substance or alcohol abuse, or recurrent suicide ideation or previous attempt. The sensitivity of the Columbia Teen Screen was approximately 88%, and specificity was 76%. These settings resulted in only 3 screen-negative students who met the criterion and were indeed at risk, but were not detected by the Columbia Teen Screen. In addition, there were 257 false-positive screens, which highlights the importance of being able to have a second phase to screen out those who are not actually at risk for suicide. Another finding of this work was that the problems of many adolescents who were at high risk for suicide were not known to others, and thus these students had never received any treatment. Only 31% of those who suffered from major depressive disorder, 26% of those with recent and frequent suicide ideation, and 50% of those who made a past suicide attempt were actually in treatment.

Directly screening teenagers to identify those at high risk is not only efficient, but it is also cost effective. The current cost of this screening

procedure is $37 per student screened, or just under $250 per student referred. The overall cost to screen approximately 1000 students is about
$25,000. This cost will decrease in the near future, however, as the DISC
is now being made into a spoken, self-completion (Voice DISC) version
that will eliminate the need for interviewers and also enhance outreach.
Within the year, we anticipate being able to go into a high school, dis-
tribute the Columbia Teen Screen, and then set up an entire classroom
with laptop computers complete with headphones, enabling 20 to 25 students to independently complete the DISC interview at the same time.
Not only will the Voice DISC cut costs, it will also increase the rate at
which teenagers can be screened, thus making the screening process even
more efficient and succinct. With these technological advances, it will be
possible to incorporate this screening method into high school health
evaluations that are already routinely conducted.

Current trends in adolescent suicide

The most recent adolescent suicide statistics available may give cause for
encouragement. White males have historically held the highest suicide
rate. In recent decades, their rate began a 23-year increase in 1965, reaching a peak in 1987, at which point it remained fairly constant for several
years.

An exciting change occurred in 1996, though, and the white-male suicide rate evinced a dramatic and inexplicable reduction. One possible explanation for this decrease is a natural periodicity that is not fully under-
stood. Another explanation is that an alcohol or drug effect on the
elevation of the suicide rate coincided with an increase in the rate of alcohol exposure during this period. There is some evidence that substance-
and alcohol-use, although not abuse, rates are dropping, and this change
could account for the decreasing male suicide rate. Another possible explanation is that we could be seeing the effects of therapeutic treatment.
Prior to 1992, adolescent depression was rarely treated with tricyclics due
to their known side effects, lethality at even modest overdose levels, and
low compliance rates. Today, however, selective serotonin reuptake inhibitor (SSRI) antidepressants are prescribed with increasing frequency,
and the reduction in the suicide rate could be a direct result of this change
in treatment strategy.

14

Lawmakers Must Act to Prevent Teen Suicide

Julie Thomerson

Julie Thomerson is a former National Conference of State Legislatures specialist in youth violence and delinquency.

Youth suicide is a growing epidemic. However, there are a variety of ways that state legislatures can support practitioners, school officials, and parents trying to reduce teen suicide rates. State legislatures may improve the school environment so students feel more connected and supported. Legislatures can also fund after-school programs, which can keep children out of trouble as well as provide screening programs to detect early signs of suicidal behavior. Eighteen states already have youth suicide prevention laws, but tight budgets make funding these programs a challenge. The economic toll of youth suicide makes the investment more than worthwhile, however.

More teenagers and young adults die from suicide each year than from cancer, heart disease, AIDS, birth defects, stroke, pneumonia, influenza and chronic lung disease combined. The sad reality is that youth suicide is a growing epidemic, ending young lives and leaving heartbroken families and communities. It is currently the third leading cause of death of 15- to 24-year-olds, and the fourth leading cause of death among 10- to 14-year-olds. Nearly 4,600 kids killed themselves in the United States in 1998, and approximately 46,000 others tried. Most give warnings; some do not.

Teenage suicides seldom make the front pages. Or do they? Andrew Wurst, 14, talked to his friends about taking his own life a month before he shot and killed a teacher and wounded three students at a high school dance. Luke Woodham, 16, told investigators that he shot nine students—killing two—because he was so miserable that he "just couldn't take it anymore." He later confessed that he had wanted to die. Another teenager who had already attempted suicide asked his parents for a gun. They gave it to him. Soon after, he took it to school, wounded a fellow student, then shot and killed himself.

More recently, Jason Anthony Hoffman took a firearm and wounded five at Granite Hills High School in San Diego. He then hanged himself in jail. He had a history of mental illness and was taking antidepressants months before the shooting.

"Without exception, every juvenile I've represented in a murder case has tried to kill himself," said Hoffman's attorney, William Lafond. "Many of these kids feel helpless and depressed and don't understand why they did what they did. When they try to understand their feelings, they can't handle it."

More teenagers and young adults die from suicide each year than from cancer, heart disease, AIDS, birth defects, stroke, pneumonia, influenza and chronic lung disease combined.

Research shows that up to 60 percent of school shooters may have been suicidal before they shot others, and a majority of them gave clues. Most had a history of depression and were desperate to end their emotional pain, and many communicated their agony to someone else in some way. They directed their aggression toward more than just those who hurt them. They had specific targets: themselves.

No one means to absolve these kids from responsibility for their horrific acts. They usually planned ahead, knew what they were doing, had given up on life and were not concerned about the consequences. And most planned to kill themselves before they were done.

"I didn't really see my life going on any further," Luke Woodham now says. "I thought it was all over with . . . I couldn't find a reason not to do it."

We focus more on troubled children killing others than the thousands of children privately taking their lives every year. In reality, youth violence is a tremendous problem, and suicide is a big part of it. For lawmakers, the questions are how to design policies to prevent young people from getting to this point of desperation, and how to intervene when they do.

What is going on?

Suicide among children ages 10 to 14 increased nearly 100 percent between 1981 and 1998, jumping from 163 deaths per 100,000 to 317, according to the Centers for Disease Control. Suicide among African American males ages 15 to 19 rose at an even higher rate, increasing from 81 deaths per 100,000 to 164. One youth commits suicide every two hours in the United States.

There are several theories about why this happens. One is that some children are growing up without meaningful connections to adults or the support they need to successfully navigate the process of growing up. Another is that kids are impulsive and can react to a moment of crisis in their lives—such as trouble in school, relationship problems or bullying—without stopping to really think about consequences. In some cases, impulsive behavior and access to guns is a dangerous mixture. Others blame substance abuse, media violence or copycat actions.

Depression is one of the most common problems children and adolescents face, says Mark Weist, director of the Center for School Mental Health Assistance in Baltimore, Md. "Often, mental health issues in youth are not identified, especially if they are less observable problems like depression and anxiety."

Statistics show that one in 10 young people suffers from mental illness serious enough to be impaired, but fewer than 20 percent receive treatment. Many, especially boys, keep their problems to themselves and do not seek help unless an adult intervenes. Others live in communities without mental health services or their parents distrust the help that is available.

Colorado Representative Kay Alexander points out that 80 percent of kids with mental health problems also abuse alcohol or drugs. "They are often either self-medicating or the substance abuse contributes to their mental health problems," she says.

"Mental health providers need support in raising awareness, destigmatizing mental illness and treating mental health as equal in importance to physical health," says Weist. "Since [the terrorist attacks of September 11, 2001], there is an increased awareness that mental health issues are universal. Hopefully, this will translate into more resources for effective child and adolescent mental health programs."

For lawmakers, the questions are how to design policies to prevent young people from getting to this point of desperation, and how to intervene when they do.

Part of the problem is that troubled kids often appear to be "normal," well-adjusted students, says Weist. When 15-year-old Charles Bishop ended his life by crashing a Cessna airplane into a Tampa office building in January, he had given no indication beforehand that he intended to hurt himself. And 16-year-old Jason Flatt was a popular boy with a supportive family. No one expected him to shoot and kill himself in 1997 after breaking up with his girlfriend.

"Many boys have an exterior structure that looks healthy and happy, but behind it lies more pain than we can imagine. Often, they either feel too ashamed to talk about it or have no one they can really talk to. And they usually show signs beforehand, even if no one notices," says William Pollack, acclaimed Harvard psychologist, director of the Centers for Men and Young Men, and author of *Real Boys* and *Real Boys' Voices*.

What can legislatures do?

"We need to understand all the issues around why people attempt suicide," says Oklahoma Representative Darrell Gilbert. "The more we learn, the easier it is to design policy change current laws and appropriate dollars to help with the problem."

The bottom line is that the problems are too complex for any simple solution. There is no single description of a suicidal child, and no way to make sure kids never kill themselves. But there are a variety of ways that legislatures can support practitioners, school officials and parents.

One need is more education about the risk factors for youth suicide. If teachers, parents, coaches, students and others know how to recognize the warning signs for suicide, they may have more opportunities to ask questions, listen, solve problems or aid kids in getting help. "Kids do not wake up suddenly suicidal; they get there after traveling down a long road," says Richard Lieberman, Los Angeles school psychologist. "Where we intercept these kids on the road determines what our response should be."

The bottom line is that the problems are too complex for any simple solution. There is no single description of a suicidal child, and no way to make sure kids never kill themselves.

Each state may have different needs that can be addressed through legislation. In some cases, schools might be directed to run programs where kids role-play difficult situations and talk about better ways to work through conflict or cope with disappointment. Preliminary findings of one study suggest that mentally healthy students who practice solving life problems through role-playing with other students are less likely to get depressed or show signs of suicidal behavior. "We need funding and personnel for prevention programs in schools to teach kids valuable coping skills so that they don't travel down the path to begin with," Lieberman says.

Another approach is to improve the school environment so students feel more connected and supported. Staff can be trained to mentor children better and to stop bullying and conflict more effectively. Classes can be smaller so students get more attention and know each other better. Kids can be trained to mediate conflicts between peers.

After-school programs can also help kids stay out of trouble, learn new skills and improve their self-esteem. Some schools also take time during the school day to teach kids about suicide, although some researchers argue that this approach leads kids to think about it as an alternative when they did not before.

Other suggestions include funding mental health services for troubled students, requiring professional screening of students for early signs of suicidal behavior and restricting access to firearms.

Where lawmakers need to make the most of limited funds, it is important to make sure that prevention programs are effective and a good investment of state money. There is some research that implies that the aforementioned efforts can help reduce suicidal behavior. At the same time, there is little hard proof that individual programs are effective, even though schools report they are helping. Some researchers also suggest that certain programs may be counterproductive—such as suicide awareness—but no real data exists to show a negative impact. As a result, states can work toward ensuring better investments by requiring assessment of state-funded prevention programs.

What are states doing?

At this point we know that comprehensive, broad-based approaches are the most successful at preventing youth suicide. They include everyone—professionals from different disciplines, community agencies, parents, kids and others—in efforts to coordinate services, share resources and work together to help kids deal with the problems that may lead them to become suicidal. Basically, the comprehensive approach intervenes early to help young people overcome barriers to development and learning and grow up successfully.

Eighteen states have youth suicide prevention laws, and many have worked to put fairly comprehensive approaches in place. Washington uses general funds to educate the public about youth suicide and staff a 24-hour crisis hotline. Other states—Kentucky, Florida, New York, New Jersey, Connecticut, Hawaii and Maryland—fund school-based mental health programs for troubled students, including suicide risks. Louisiana is developing a statewide youth suicide prevention plan.

Oklahoma recently established a Youth Suicide Prevention Council to collaborate with community organizations, develop local resources, provide technical assistance to community programs, make policy recommendations to the Legislature and promote public awareness. The Legislature was responding to increased incidents and rising concern in Oklahoma, says Representative Gilbert, co-sponsor of the law. Lawmakers wanted to include various perspectives in planning a prevention policy, since "the more information we can find out about why teens are committing suicide, the more we can help mental health professionals and others—such as religious leaders and drug and alcohol counselors—to help kids with the emotional issues in their lives," he says.

Virginia and California passed new legislation in 2001 to supplement school-based prevention programs already in place. The Virginia Department of Health is now coordinating prevention activities throughout the commonwealth. California established a statewide suicide prevention week, recognizing it as a major public health concern, declaring it a state priority and encouraging development of treatment that works, including affordable mental health care. California legislators "wanted to increase awareness and move us toward comprehensive suicide prevention plans," says bill sponsor Senator Deborah Ortiz.

California's existing school-based prevention program includes training parents and school staff about the warning signs, providing a crisis hotline for kids and developing peer support groups. "We need to direct the resources to the schools," Ortiz says. "School personnel are the most likely to run across kids who are at risk for suicide where many others may not have enough knowledge or awareness to intervene."

Barriers to intervention

One challenge is that all these solutions require money, creating a balancing act for state legislatures with limited budgets. But research points to prevention as a long-term investment due to the emotional and economic toll that suicide takes on the population. Aside from the loss of lifetime contributions when a citizen dies prematurely, emergency room use for suicide attempts costs states an average of $33,000 per visit. With approximately 730,000 attempted suicides per year nationwide that can be a pretty hefty price tag. To some degree, federal resources—such as Medicaid and the Maternal Child Health Block Grant—can help states pay for more prevention initiatives, but reimbursements can be difficult. And there is still some question whether and how much the state should be involved in these issues.

Senator Ortiz suggests that "it may take work to realize that there are successful programs out there, but it will take long-term, sustained resources to build awareness. We can save money by investing in prevention, but it is a hard case to make in difficult fiscal times."

Other challenges—such as the general stigma surrounding mental illness services—can make it harder for children and their families to get treatment or take part in prevention activities. Many are afraid that their information will not be kept confidential. Parents may also feel that life and death are family matters that should not be addressed at school. School officials also have a limited duty to protect students from harm and may be concerned about liability issues, especially if prevention efforts are ineffective.

"The challenge is to intervene, to get these kids what they need, and they need to be connected to different systems for different problems," says Iowa Representative Ro Foege. "Because of the variety of issues, the team approach is important. But the team needs to include parents, counselors, school nurses, social workers, community organizations and all others who deal with behavioral health. Everyone needs to come together to address the issue instead of being so fragmented."

Why now?

Being scared and unhappy can be part of growing up. But when it gets too hard and they do not know how to cope, unhappy kids often act out their feelings—sometimes by hurting themselves or others. Suicide is ultimately a mental health problem, but there are triggers and contributing factors that lead young people to turn to suicide as a solution, rather than dealing with their problems in healthier ways.

"It is alarming that we live in a time when so many teenagers feel they have nowhere to turn," says Texas Representative Geanie Morrison. "As a society, we must do more to provide a safety net and let these children know that this is a terminal solution to a temporary problem."

There is no doubt that youth suicide is a tragic act of self-violence that wreaks havoc on the lives of young people and those they leave behind. "We have to look beyond whether we are saving money," says Montana Representative Paul Clark. "We are talking about kids' lives. We are also talking about the health of our families and society. Increases in suicidal behavior should be a red flag for legislatures."

Organizations to Contact

The editors have compiled the following list of organizations concerned with the issues debated in this book. The descriptions are derived from materials provided by the organizations. All have publications or information available for interested readers. The list was compiled on the date of publication of the present volume; names, addresses, phone and fax numbers, and e-mail addresses may change. Be aware that many organizations take several weeks or longer to respond to inquiries, so allow as much time as possible.

American Academy of Child and Adolescent Psychiatry
3615 Wisconsin Ave. NW, Washington, DC 20016-3007
(202) 966-7300 • fax: (202) 966-2891
Web site: www.aacap.org

The American Academy of Child and Adolescent Psychiatry is a professional medical organization made up of child and adolescent psychiatrists trained to promote healthy development and to evaluate, diagnose, and treat children and adolescents and their families who are affected by disorders of feeling, thinking, and behavior. Child and adolescent psychiatrists are physicians who are uniquely qualified to integrate knowledge about human behavior and development from biological, psychological, familial, social, and cultural perspectives with scientific, humanistic, and collaborative approaches to diagnosis, treatment, and the promotion of mental health. It publishes the *Journal of the American Academy of Child and Adolescent Psychiatry*.

American Association of Suicidology (AAS)
4201 Connecticut Ave. NW, Suite 408, Washington, DC 20008
(202) 237-2280 • National Hopeline Network: 1-800-SUICIDE
Web site: www.suicidology.org

The American Association of Suicidology focuses on the understanding and prevention of suicide. AAS promotes research, public awareness programs, public education, and training for professionals and volunteers. In addition, AAS serves as a national clearinghouse for information on suicide. The membership of AAS includes mental health and public health professionals, researchers, suicide prevention and crisis intervention centers, school districts, crisis center volunteers, survivors of suicide, and a variety of laypersons who have an interest in suicide prevention. It publishes *Suicide and Life-Threatening Behavior*, AAS's quarterly journal; *Newslink*, a quarterly newsletter for members; and *Surviving Suicide*, a quarterly newsletter for survivors.

American Foundation for Suicide Prevention
120 Wall St., 22nd Floor, New York, NY 10005
(212) 363-3500 • (888) 333-AFSP • fax: (212) 363-6237
e-mail: inquiry@afsp.org • Web site: www.afsp.org

The American Foundation for Suicide Prevention is dedicated to advancing knowledge of suicide and the ability to prevent it. The foundation's activities include supporting research projects that help further the understanding of depression and the prevention of suicide; providing information about depression and suicide; promoting professional education for the recognition and treatment of depressed and suicidal individuals; publicizing the magnitude of the problem and the need for research, prevention, and treatment; and supporting programs for suicide survivor treatment, research, and education. It publishes a newsletter, *Lifesavers*, and has produced an educational video entitled "The Suicidal Patient: Assessment and Care."

American Psychiatric Association
1000 Wilson Blvd., Suite 1825, Arlington, VA 22209-3901
(703) 907-7322 • (800) 368-5777 • fax: (703) 907-1091
e-mail: appi@psych.org • Web site: www.psych.org

The American Psychiatric Association is a medical specialty society recognized worldwide. Its thirty-seven thousand U.S. and international member physicians work together to ensure humane care and effective treatment for all persons with mental disorders, including mental retardation and substance-related disorders. Its vision is a society that has available, accessible quality psychiatric diagnosis and treatment. American Psychiatric Publishing publishes the *American Journal of Psychiatry* as well as numerous other more specialized psychiatric journals.

Australian Institute for Suicide Research and Prevention (AISRAP)
Griffith University, Mt. Gravatt Campus
Brisbane, Queensland 4111, Australia
07-3875-3377 • fax: 07-3875-3450
e-mail: aisrap@griffith.edu.au • Web site: www.griffith.edu.au/aisrap

The institute is part of Griffith University's ongoing commitment toward better public health for all Australians. The aim of the Australian Institute for Suicide Research and Prevention is to promote, conduct, and support comprehensive programs of research activities for the prevention of suicidal behaviors in Australia. AISRAP's Suicide Prevention Skills Training Workshops provide a complete knowledge and skills-based approach to suicide prevention training across prevention, intervention, and postvention. The workshop has been developed for individuals working within a broad range of fields including health, education, emergency, clergy, law enforcement, community, and social services. The institute publishes the *Suicide Prevention Skills Trainer's Manual*.

Canadian Association for Suicide Prevention (CASP)
c/o The Support Network
11456 Jasper Ave., #301, Edmonton, AB T5K 0M1 Canada
(780) 482-0198 • fax: (780) 488-1495
e-mail: casp@suicideprevention.ca • Web site: www.suicideprevention.ca

The Canadian Association for Suicide Prevention was incorporated in 1985 by a group of professionals who saw the need to provide information and resources to the community at large to reduce the suicide rate and minimize the harmful consequences of suicidal behavior. CASP's ultimate purpose is to reduce the suicide rate and minimize the harmful consequences of suicidal behavior. CASP works toward the achievement of its purpose by facilitating, advocating, supporting, and advising, rather than by the provision of direct services. CASP publishes brochures, including "What Can I Do? . . . If I Suspect That Someone I Know Is Suicidal?" and "Living with Someone Who Is Suicidal."

Centre for Suicide Prevention
1202 Centre St. SE, Suite 320, Calgary, AB T2G 5A5 Canada
(403) 245-3900 • fax: (403) 245-0299
e-mail: siec@suicideinfo.ca • Web site: www.suicideinfo.ca

The Centre for Suicide Prevention has three main branches. The Suicide Information & Education Collection (SIEC) is a special library and resource center providing information on suicide and suicidal behavior. The Suicide Prevention Training Programs (SPTP) branch provides caregiver training in suicide intervention, awareness, bereavement, crisis management, and related topics. Suicide Prevention Research Projects (SPRP) advocates for and supports research on suicide and suicidal behavior.

Depression and Bipolar Support Alliance (DBSA)
730 N. Franklin St., Suite 501, Chicago, IL 60610-7204
(800) 826-3632 • fax: (312) 642-7243
Web site: www.dbsalliance.org

The Depression and Bipolar Support Alliance is the nation's leading patient-directed organization focusing on the most prevalent mental illnesses—depression and bipolar disorder. The organization fosters an understanding about the impact and management of these life-threatening illnesses by providing up-to-date, scientifically based tools and information written in language the general public can understand. DBSA supports research to promote more timely diagnosis, develop more effective and tolerable treatments, and discover a cure. The organization works to ensure that people living with mood disorders are treated equitably. It has published several books, including *How I Stayed Alive When My Brain Was Trying to Kill Me* as well as several brochures about bipolar disorder and suicide.

National Mental Health Association (NMHA)
2001 N. Beauregard St., 12th Floor, Alexandria, VA 22311
(703) 684-7722 • (800) 969-6642 • fax: (703) 684-5968
Web site: www.nmha.org

The National Mental Health Association is the country's oldest and largest nonprofit organization addressing all aspects of mental health and mental illness. With more than 340 affiliates nationwide, NMHA works to improve the mental health of all Americans, especially the 54 million individuals with mental disorders, through advocacy, education, research, and service. It publishes a pamphlet entitled *What Is Depression?*

NIMH Suicide Research Consortium
National Institute of Mental Health (NIMH), Office of Communications
6001 Executive Blvd., Room 8184, MSC 9663, Bethesda, MD 20892-9663
(301) 443-4513 • (866) 615-6464 • fax: (301) 443-4279
e-mail: nimhinfo@nih.gov • Web site: www.nimh.nih.gov

The NIMH Suicide Research Consortium is comprised primarily of NIMH scientists across the institute who also administer research grants. The consortium coordinates program development in suicide research across the institute, identifies gaps in the scientific knowledge base on suicide across the life span; stimulates and monitors extramural research on suicide; keeps abreast of scientific developments in suicidology and public policy issues related to suicide surveillance, prevention, and treatment; and disseminates science-based information on suicidology to the public, media, and policy makers. Its Web site contains statistics, research links, and research funding opportunities.

Suicide Awareness Voices of Education (SAVE)
7317 Cahill Rd., Suite 207, Minneapolis, MN 55439-2080
(952) 946-7998
e-mail: save@save.org • Web site: www.save.org

The mission of SAVE is to educate the public about suicide prevention, eliminate the stigma associated with suicide, and support those touched by suicide. SAVE is committed to the education of the general public about the depressive brain diseases such as clinical depression and bipolar illness that can result in suicide if left untreated medically and psychologically. The organization is largely made up of suicide survivors and people who have suffered from depression. The major event for the organization is SAVE's annual Suicide Awareness and Memorial Day, which is held every spring in Minneapolis, Minnesota, and draws nearly five hundred people. It publishes a newsletter *Voices of SAVE*.

Teenage Suicide.com
4763 Main St., Suite 2-a, Seattle, WA 60042
(206) 312-4760
e-mail: info@1-teenage-suicide.com • Web site: www.1-teenage-suicide.com

This organization was created by the parents of a teenage suicide victim. It contains statistics; links to other organizations; advice for parents, including the warning signs of possible teen suicide and what actions to take to prevent it; and resources for depressed teens. It is associated with the Jed Foundation, a nonprofit organization committed to reducing the youth suicide rate and improving the mental health support provided by universities to students nationwide. The foundation is currently working with advocacy groups such as the National Mental Health Association, leading psychiatrists, and mental health professionals to help further the foundation's goals.

University of Oxford Centre for Suicide Research
Department of Psychiatry
Warneford Hospital, Oxford, OX3 7JX United Kingdom
44 (0)1865 226258 • fax: 44 (0)1865 223933
e-mail: csr@psychiatry.ox.ac.uk • Web site: www.psychiatry.ox.ac.uk

The research conducted by the University of Oxford Centre for Suicide Research encompasses both suicide and attempted suicide. The research program includes epidemiological studies and investigation of the full range of the causes of suicidal behavior—psychological, psychiatric, social, and biological. It is especially interested in developing and evaluating effective methods of treating people after suicide attempts and preventing suicidal behavior. It is also concerned with improving care for bereaved relatives and other people affected by suicide. The Web site includes an index of all department faculty publications.

Yellow Ribbon Suicide Prevention Program
PO Box 644, Westminster, CO 80036-0644
(303) 429-3530 • fax: (303) 426-4496
e-mail: Ask4help@yellowribbon.org • Web site: www.yellowribbon.org

Yellow Ribbon offers a comprehensive suicide prevention program for schools and communities. Its training seminars are cost-effective, user friendly, and easy to understand. Yellow Ribbon's Be-A-Link Gatekeeper presentations and training are available to youth and adults. Its curricula are designed for lay-people as well as professionals, and EMS/fire and law enforcement personnel. Yellow Ribbon chapters, schools, and other organizations throughout the United States and forty-seven countries use its collaborative program.

Bibliography

Books

Alan Carr	*Depression and Attempted Suicide in Adolescence.* Malden, MA: BPS Blackwell, 2002.
Bev Cobain	*When Nothing Matters Anymore: A Survival Guide for Depressed Teens.* Minneapolis, MN: Free Spirit, 1998.
Kay R. Jamison	*Night Falls Fast: Understanding Suicide.* New York: Knopf, 1999.
Miriam Kaufman	*Overcoming Teen Depression: A Guide for Parents.* Buffalo, NY: Firefly Books, 2001.
James M. Murphy	*Coping with Teen Suicide.* New York: Rosen, 1999.
Judith Peacock	*Teen Suicide.* Mankato, MN: LifeMatters, 2000.
Jessica Portner	*One in Thirteen: The Silent Epidemic of Teen Suicide.* Beltsville, MD: Robins Lane Press, 2001.
Paul R. Robbins	*Adolescent Suicide.* Jefferson, NC: McFarland, 1998.
Jay Schleifer	*Everything You Need to Know About Teen Suicide.* New York: Rosen, 1999.
Nicole B. Sperekas	*Suicide Wise: Taking Steps Against Teen Suicide.* Berkeley Heights, NJ: Enslow, 2000.
Anthony Spirito and James C. Overholser, eds.	*Evaluating and Treating Adolescent Suicide Attempters: From Research to Practice.* Boston: Academic Press, 2003.
Claire Wallerstein	*Teen Suicide.* Chicago: Heinemann Library, 2003.

Periodicals

Daniel Close and John Allcott	"Teen Suicide Focuses on Firearms," *Register Guard,* May 9, 2002.
Wilhelmina J. Drummond	"Adolescents at Risk: Causes of Youth Suicide in New Zealand," *Adolescence,* Winter 1997.
Economist	"Why Do So Many Young Americans End Their Own Lives?" December 8, 2001.
Robert M. Fernquist	"Problem Drinking in the Family and Youth Suicide," *Adolescence,* Fall 2000.
Gordon Harper	"Teen Depression: Overlooked and Undertreated," *Patient Care,* October 2002.
Keith A. King	"Student Suicide Prevention Begins with Recognition," *School Administrator,* May 2000.

Lancet	"SSRIs: Suicide Risk and Withdrawal," June 14, 2003.
Anna Mulrine	"Preventing Teen Suicide: It Starts with Straight Talk," *U.S. News & World Report*, December 20, 1999.
Iain Murray	"When It Comes to Suicide, Gun Control Is Not the Answer," *St. Louis Post-Dispatch*, December 14, 1999.
Pediatrics	"Suicide and Suicide Attempts in Adolescents," April 2000.
Mary Desmond Pinkowish	"Panic Attacks Increase Suicide Risk in Adolescence," *Patient Care*, January 15, 2000.
Monica Preboth	"AAP Statement on Suicide in Adolescents," *American Family Physician*, December 15, 2000.
Jim Rosack	"Suicide Prevention Advocates Emphasize New Strategies," *Psychiatric News*, April 7, 2000.
Philip A. Rutter and Emil Soucar	"Youth Suicide Risk and Sexual Orientation," *Adolescence*, Summer 2002.
James U. Scott	"Teasing and Bullying: What Can Pediatricians Do?" *Contemporary Pediatrics*, April 2003.
Christopher K. Varley	"Don't Overlook Depression in Youth," *Contemporary Pediatrics*, January 2002.
David Wilkins and Jane DeVille-Almond	"Action to Prevent Male Suicide," *Practice Nurse*, September 12, 2003.
Alan J. Zametkin, Marisa R. Alter, and Tamar Yemini	"Suicide in Teenagers: Assessment, Management, and Prevention," *Journal of the American Medical Association*, December 26, 2001.

Internet Sources

David A. Brent	"Bipolar Disorder and Youth Suicide," American Foundation for Suicide Prevention. www.afsp.org.
David A. Brent	"Familial Factors in Suicide and Suicidal Behavior," American Foundation for Suicide Prevention. www.afsp.org.
Brown University Child and Adolescent Psychopharmacology Update	"Medication May Help Prevent Suicide in Teens," March 2003. www.medscape.com/viewarticle/450638.
Dave Kopel	"The Fallacy of '43 to 1'," *National Review Online*, January 31, 2001. www.nationalreview.com.

Index